INTERVIEW WITH A ZOO KEEPER

COLIN NORTHCOTT

Follow me on Twitter and Instagram, or subscribe to my YouTube channel for additional stories and updates.

csfn_me@yahoo.co.uk
Twitter: @csfnorthcott
Instagram: cnorthcott64

Front cover: Author, Colin with 'Safari' the Cheetah. 1990. ©
Back cover: Sunset on the Savannah at West Midland Safari
              Park. © Colin Northcott.

Dedicated to all the animals I have worked with over the years and to all the special people who have dedicated their lives in to looking after them.

Special thanks to my good friend Liam Smith for the interviews and for giving me the kick start and assistance I needed to write this book.

Also to Andria Johns, Vicky Grice and Helen Slade for their time, advice and support.

PROLOGUE

I have worked with exotic animals for almost all of my working life. It's impossible to work with dangerous creatures without things happening, both good and bad. This is a record, or a memoir if you like, of some of the antics and events that have happened to me before, and during my career. Some of it in anecdotal form so it is as candid and as casual as possible. Some names may have been changed to respect their privacy.

Interviews with Liam Smith. Our conversations were integral in sparking memories and guiding me on writing this book. We chewed the fat whilst chewing on a carvery at the local pub.

A single memory can spark another, and another and so on, until, before you know it, you have a book.

I hope you enjoy reading it.

CHAPTERS

CHAPTER 1

A chat in the pub

Up to the point of writing this book I have worked within the zoo industry for over 33 years and in almost every role within the usual running of an animal collection, from Keeper to Curator. Something I have always wanted to do since my school days. Born in Cardiff, Wales, I moved to Plymouth in Devon at the age of five when my family relocated. This is when my real interest in animals started. Living close to the now closed Plymouth zoo I used to visit often and see, in wonderment, all the incredible animals within it. And so I set out to travel a long road to becoming part of this incredible industry.

My memories and stories are as I recall them from various conversations and banter with my family and friends over many years. They are not necessarily in chronological order, but they are incites into my life and my career within the Zoological world.

Liam, my good friend and once colleague, who's sense of humour and caring nature kept me sane on many occasions. He always took an interest in my stories and is integral in giving me that big push to put pen to paper.

"So"...

I laugh. "This is a bit odd!" Liam says, "This is a bit weird isn't it. We've just got to ignore it." I replied.

Being in a restaurant to conduct an interview is odd to us, although it makes perfect sense. To be in a relaxed atmosphere allows us both to be candid and have fun. Having a good meal throughout was a bonus.

I took my pen and note pad with me with the intention of making notes throughout the afternoon.... I didn't use them!

I have known Liam for a while by now and his first question to me was to ask why I decided to get in to this industry in the first place, and was there anything specific that made me decide to pursue my animal career?

It was a multitude of things that really caught my attention. Watching Johnny Morris, who presented 'Animal Magic' on the television, and going to the Plymouth Zoo played a big role in influencing me towards what I do now.

I will never forget seeing the infamous 'Percy' the Pelican who was allowed to roam free around the zoo. He would often sit on a fence rail and steal your popcorn, or follow children around and pull on their jumpers. I was completely taken by him. He gained lots of notoriety at Central Park Zoo in Plymouth. I also remember seeing a keeper with a Lion cub. He was allowing kids stroke it and, of course, I had to get in on the act. An amazing experience. Todays modern zoos no longer allow this kind of interaction very often, and rightly so.

There was also a huge Hippo who lived on the outer edge of the perimeter. She could be seen from the public footpath outside the zoo and I would often walk past her enclosure just to take a look. She would invariably be in her mud wallow and all you could see of her was the ridge of her back. If she defecated she would flick it up high in to the air and it would fall like a rain shower of shite! Huge amounts of amusement for a child. I realise now, that conditions at this zoo were far from ideal, but back then animal welfare and husbandry was not considered very high on the priority list. It seems that commercialism was higher. Of course you need the visitor funding to pay for the running but nothing appeared to be spent on furthering improvements to the infrastructure or on animal care and welfare.

Moving to Somerset and joining the Young Ornithologist Club, (YOC), also played a big part. I put up bird tables in my garden and started to learn about the birds that visited. I still use the same bird book I got when I was 12 years old. I do have quite a collection of bird books now but I can't help reverting back to my original first book.

My first organised trip to see any wildlife was just after I turned 13 and with the YOC. We went out to Chew Valley Lake in Somerset. I knew very little about birds but that was about to change. The first bird I saw that wasn't 'a little brown job' was an Avocet. A beautiful wading bird with a long, upward curved beak. They are also the logo of the RSPB. Hence forth my interest in birds really took off. (See what I did there?). I was hooked.

Spending much of my free time walking around the local area I started to learn more and more about the wildlife around me. Influenced by Johnny Morris and David Attenborough my appetite for working with animals just kept growing.

I must have been boring Liam to sleep but he listened to my

stories and between us my memories grew more and more vivid, as I tucked into my amazing roast turkey dinner.

We continued to reminisce about my childhood influences and my desire to work with animals. So much so that I started to tell him about the time my next door neighbour and myself decided we would set up a rescue centre. We called it the Animal Rescue Centre, (ARC). I know, pretty original huh! Our first mission was soon upon us. Before I tell you what it was please remember we were only kids about 12 years old, with a pretty weird sense of humour! By now Liam is gripped.

I found a dead mouse, which was a bit late to rescue I reckon. But we decided to give it a funeral. We lived by the river so it was going to be a burial at, well, sea. It would end up in the sea eventually, or so we assumed. I found a stick and laid the Mouse on it. I had an old Union Flag handkerchief so I draped it over the corpse and between us we carried it, on our shoulders, up to the bridge.

We got some very odd looks from the passers by, and rightly so. Between the giggles we said a few words and slid the Mouse from under the flag and watched him drop to the icy depths below. Except he floated. Not sure we had thought this through properly. We both laughed as we watched our failure slowly drift off down the river towards the sea.

Even though this was just a bit of weird fun it was still part of the bigger picture for my desire to work with and help animals.

'Percy'
Central Park Zoo. Plymouth. Circa 1970's
Picture courtesy of Derek Tait.

CHAPTER 2

Lets get started

I left school with no real idea what I was going to do for a living. However, all the time in the back of my mind, I know I wanted to work with animals in some form or another. I started just to write to every zoo and wildlife park in the country and see what came up. This was not easy when I had no access to a photocopier or any form of device to assist me. I remember sitting in our kitchen looking at a blank page wondering how to start. With no real qualifications behind me, I didn't hold much hope that this would work. I also knew that if I didn't try then my dreams had even less chance. So I started writing. Short and sweet and to the point was the order of the day. So my pen hit the paper.

Several hours, or it may have been days later, I had myself a large pile of letters ready to post. Now it was just a case of sitting back and waiting for the job offers to come flooding in.

I already had a job at a small animal feed warehouse next door to my home. I was enjoying it but it wasn't really what I wanted to do. Living on the Somerset levels I had a huge area of fantastic countryside to satisfy my desire for nature. I could sit by the river and watch Kingfishers and Herons and one day even a Mink came up to me. I froze in disbelief that such a creature would come so close. It came up to my foot and sniffed my boot. I could hardly breathe. It's encounters like this that cemented my desire to work with animals.

Not far from home was a large Heronry. I went there with a close friend and we could see the chicks in the trees squawking away for their parents attention. Such large birds on the slimmest of branches seemed almost impossible. I was determined to make animals my living, somehow.

Every day I would wait for the postman. Every morning there was nothing for me. Weeks turned to months and by now I was beginning to realise that I was not going to get anything anytime soon. Surely I didn't have to write the same letter every month! Finding advertised positions was nearly impossible. With real despondency I pretty much gave up on my dream to work with wild animals. Maybe I gave up too easily but hindsight is a wonderful thing. And no good to you when you've already set your path.

I settled with continuing to working at the warehouse and getting my wildlife fix on my days off. It was fine though. I did enjoy it. Months turned to years and so it went on. Then a change in my circumstances forced a sudden move away from home. It isn't fair to be bringing up old events that involve other people, who do not have a platform to reply, so I will leave you with a tantalising nugget of intrigue and keep you wondering. Sorry. (Not).

By this time my parents had moved away and I found myself living with a friend in order to stay in Somerset.

However, I was forced to relocate and so I did the usual young adult thing and moved back in with my parents, only this time, it was in Slough in Berkshire.

I found a job with delivering stationary in and around London. A world away from what I wanted as my ideal job. From remote countryside to Britains capitol city was not what I had planned to do with my life. Not that I had a clear plan in the first place, but I knew working in London as a driver couldn't be any further from my original career goal of working with wild animals. But needs must and I had to earn a living somehow, and somewhere.

Working from a base in Bermondsey I travelled daily in and out of London and was definitely not enjoying the rat race life. But after just a few months the company went bust! That was all I needed. Now out of work, I was beginning to despair. But not one to sit on my heels, I found another company to work for just a few streets from my parents home. This was so much better than commuting into and out of London on a daily basis. The job was still the same but this time I was delivering across the home counties, so better than the London traffic I guess. But the animal kingdom was never far away from my thoughts and I had to try again to get in to the industry somehow.

When I first moved up to Slough I couldn't help but notice that not far from me was the Windsor Safari Park. The next step was obvious. I had to write to them and see if there was any chance of work within the animal department. I was elated when they wrote back and invited me for an interview. I just couldn't believe it. I donned my only suit and hurried off to the park with butterflies having a house party in my stomach. I took the interview with the parks Curator. He asked me if I had any animal work experience. I had none, but I told him how passionate I was about my desire to work with them and, embarrassingly, I went on to tell him my dead mouse story. Oh well, it was too late now. I came away with no real idea how well I had done, or if I had been completely useless. All I could do was wait. Weeks went by and I heard nothing. So I continued with the delivering of pens and paper and stationary paraphernalia to whoever needed it. I enjoyed the driving and I did get to see a lot of countryside. It was better than driving in London. Being able to see green fields and passing birds was definitely preferable to the seemingly endless concrete jungle. Then, one day, completely out of the blue......

...I arrived home on the Friday afternoon after a long week of deliveries, when my mother told me that I needed to contact the Safari Park as soon as possible. I rushed for the phone and dialled the number. I got through to Paul, the Curator of animals, with whom I had the interview, and he offered me a job. Words cannot express my elation at hearing this news. Finally, my chance had come. He asked me when I could start and, without hesitation, I told him, "I'll start Monday morning if you like?" To which he agreed. We finished the phone call and I was completely blown away. Then it dawned on me what I had just done.

I have accepted my dream job but I had to give notice to my current. To make things more interesting I had the company van at home with me and it was now the weekend. There was no way I was going to miss the chance of working at the Safari Park, so I hatched a plan that, in hindsight, was probably not very professional, but to me it was the only way. I jumped straight back in to the van and drove it up to the depot. I parked it up outside the front of the building and locked it up. I wrote a note stating that I will no longer be working for the company and attached the note to the keys, then gleefully posted the lot through the letter box. As I walked home I realised that this was not really the way to do things, but it was too late. I couldn't retrieve the keys even if I wanted to. I was committed. And I was delighted. As of Monday I was going to be an exotic animal keeper.

I begin to tell Liam about starting at Windsor Safari Park. The beginning of the best ride of my life.

And so it begins......

CHAPTER 3

Lion around

It's 07:50 on Monday 28th March 1988. I rock up to the security gate of Windsor Safari Park. A rather big bearded chap asks me how he can help me and I proudly tell him that I am the new starter on the animal department. He told me where to park my car and to wait to be picked up by a park warden. Nerves are really kicking in now but soon enough a big black and white striped Land Rover pulls up. The driver say's "jump in," so I climbed in to the back. He introduces himself as "Dave, but everyone calls me Giant". Okay, I thought. I could see why. He was at least six foot six and towered over everyone. But for now, all I was concerned about was where the hell we were going. In my head, as the newbie, I'm bound to be put on pets corner or similar as I had no animal background. We drive around the corner and we're confronted with huge metal gates. Giant gets out and opens them up. Where the hell are we going?

We drove through a second set of gates and drive in to a small courtyard. "Follow me and i'll introduce you to Gunner". Gunner was the nickname of the head of this section. We walked around the corner and, oh my god! You could have knocked me down with a feather. There, right in front of me, was a long row of cages filled with Tigers and Lions. I could hardly believe my eyes. And as if to pinch me for confirmation, they started to roar. A deafening crescendo of noise that I have enjoyed every time I hear it to this day. The physical vibration of your internal organs gives you an idea of just how powerful these beasts are.

There can be no way I'm working here, I thought. Gunner came over and shook my hand. Without much more he pointed to another keeper and told me to start helping him with the cleaning. Yep. I am working here after all. Incredible!

The section not only had Lions and Tigers. There was also a mixed exhibit with Timber Wolves, Brown Bears and Black Bears. Cheetahs lived beside them and on the edge was a troop of around 130 Hamadryas Baboons along with Barbary Sheep, which I later discovered were manned by keepers on foot.

I'm reminiscing all this with Liam. "Did you have any incidents or near misses while you were there?" he asked.
"Oh definitely" I replied.

There were two three week old Lion cubs that could barely look over the side wall of their night den. I'm looking in on them and, curious as Lion cubs are, they press their noses against the mesh. Me being the rookie started to tickle the nose of one of the cubs who seemed to be enjoying it, until suddenly he snaps at my finger and catches it square across the nail and holds it tight. Although he wasn't trying to bite through he was holding it tight enough for it to hold me solid. I didn't know what to do. If I pulled away I risked tearing my finger nail off and if I stayed put I risked him finishing the job and biting the end clean off. If I called for help I risked looking like the idiot I was and getting told off in to the bargain.

Liam starts laughing. Yeah, thanks. In the course of my conundrum I was relieved when the cub decided he had had enough fun and he released his grip and set me free. I had survived my first Lion attack unscathed. Even if the cub was only 8 weeks old. It's still a Lion right! Needless to say I didn't do that again. 8 weeks or not, they can still do a lot of damage. My learning curve has started.

I hadn't been at Windsor for long when Giant decided to move on. I understand he left to work in Africa with George Adamson, famous for raising Elsa the Lion. This meant that the position of Deputy Head of Carnivores was up for grabs. The role was first offered to their keepers who had more experience than me, but they turned it down. So it finally came to me. And of course I accepted immediately.

I couldn't believe my luck. Although I was mildly terrified, but it was an opportunity I could not pass up. I was elated at the prospect. I had an amazing team and the support from the keepers was excellent. My dream was coming true.

A year or so in to my new role, I have one of the most scary incidents in my entire career. The Lion house was a large square building with dens all around it and a central covered courtyard to service the building from the inside.

When cleaning the dens it is imperative to ensure there are no Lions in them. Obviously, or so you'd think.

I walk in to the Lion house with the intention of cleaning the dens. I decided to start in one of the corner dens so I walked over to check it's availability. It's a good job I looked. The largest male Lion, 'Floyd,' is still resting in the den. He is also the pride leader. A ten year old weighing in at over 220 kilos, and has a large collection of scars to prove his claim to the throne. I open up the den beside us and Floyd walks calmly through without giving me any regard. His majesty was well above mine, and he knew it. You could hear his weight thumping on the wooden floor as if to remind you that he could crush you if he was so inclined. I lock up the hatches to make it safe for me to enter the now vacant den and I proceed to clean the den. I started in the furthest corner from the door brushing the wood shavings in to a pile. However, unknown to me, another keeper, who shall remain nameless, entered the building. He had the same intention as myself, only he decides he will start in the den to my right. The one with Floyd in! Without checking to see if my den was clear he unlocks the slide and begins to let Floyd through into my den, while I am still in it! I hear the slide open and turned around just in time to see Floyd walk in on me. With horror I froze and we both stared each stared straight into each others eyes.

I now have a huge, 220 kilogram battle scarred King of the beasts between myself and my only exit. I am now standing face to face with a Lion and the den door is open. He now has choices. He attacks me, or he walks out and escapes. What actually happens though shocked us both. I have to get out, so, broom in hand I casually walk around Floyd, my coat brushing his nose as I pass him, and step out of the den. I calmly turned and closed the door behind me. Throughout this whole manoeuvre I think Floyd was as shocked to see me in his den as I was to see him, so he just stood there, unflinching, and let me pass.

Thank goodness! Once I was safe I dropped to my knees in utter disbelief. What had just happened! Thankful that I was that Floyd had not just killed me. I wasn't as thankful to the keeper who let him in on me though. My heart still racing I made it very clear of my feelings as to what had just happened. If the lottery was available at the time I would have definitely bought a ticket that day.

My advice to anyone who works around animals that would like to have you for lunch. If you don't want to be on the menu then check, check, and check again before doing anything around them.

The lesson was learned. Any staff entering the houses of creatures who can kill you would not only check on where the animals were, but had to check where the staff were too before starting any work.

I had a new found respect for that Lion, and I feel he had my back that day. I continued to work with Floyd until he finally passed away several years later.

'Floyd'
Picture: © Colin Northcott

CHAPTER 4

Blown away

Liam was quite rightly shocked at the close call with the Lion. "Wow mate, that's amazing. You were so lucky not to be killed". He's right of course, and once again the whole incident was entirely down to human error. As was the next occasion when I have to thank my lucky stars that I'm still here to tell the tale. I hasten to add that these incidents were not a weekly event. Several years have passed between them. Liam: "So has anything else happened during your career?". "Oh yes" I replied with a wry smile.......

In the main keeper area designated for the carnivore department, were the Lion and Tiger house, the Vet room, the meat store and the food prep area. Also the staff hut where we monitored the enclosures from and, more importantly, where the tea was kept. We also had a small incinerator for the disposal of any poor critters that had passed away. We couldn't put anything heavier than a few kilo's in.

On this occasion Dan, a keeper from a different section, came over to us with a Wallaby that had just died and needed to be disposed of.

I was in the process of cleaning out the Lion house when a keeper came in and told me that a Wallaby had been brought down and asked if he could 'sort it out'. "Yes, go ahead" I replied, and I carried on sweeping. After about ten minutes, just enough time to set the thing up, he came back to me. The incinerator is powered by paper and wood so it's just a case of setting it up as if you were lighting a fire at home. "We've run out of diesel to get it started" He said. "Can I put some petrol on it?". We would sometimes use a small splash of diesel to get it going if the wood was damp, and when I say a small amount I mean about half an inch in the bottom of a paper cup so nothing too dangerous. For the 80's anyway when health and safety was not as strict as it is today! My reply though was a definite "NO, you'll have to try and light it as it is, we can't use petrol!". He walks away to try again. I continued to sweep up.

Inevitably he comes back. "I can't get it going" he says. This is where I make a big mistake. "Okay" I said, "just use a tiny splash of petrol in a cup, that'll get it started". Off he goes to light the burner and once again I get back to my sweeping. Two minutes later he's back again and says, "Do you have a lighter? I don't have mine with me". By now I'm pretty frustrated at all the interruptions for what should be a very simple task that has been done a thousand times before. In my frustration I put my brush down and tell him that I will do it. I go outside, lighter in hand, and walk up to the burner. I bend down to the open hatch and click the lighter.

BOOM!!! An almighty blast of flame comes rushing out of the chimney and, not so good for me, right out of the door directly in to my face, blowing me back against a fence about

15 feet away. I don't remember being thrown but I certainly remember everything else. My hair is on fire, my clothes are smouldering and I am very disorientated. Oddly, at this moment in time, I could feel no pain. I was so shocked I didn't really understand what had just happened. I later discovered that rather than put a splash of fuel on to light the fire he had poured about a gallon. It was inevitable what was going to happen!

Fortunately for me another keeper was hosing down the yard nearby so he rushed over and hosed me down to put out the fire. The noise of the blast was heard all over the park and the flame that went out of the chimney was like a jet fighter on after burn and was seen above the trees from the bottom of the park. Even the bosses sat in their offices heard it and the Curator was immediately on the radio trying to find out what the hell had just happened. My colleague told him that he had better come down to the Lion area immediately.

About a minute later he's on scene. He takes one look at me and without hesitation bundles me in the car and proceeds to drive, at great speed, towards the main gate. He say's "What the bloody hell happened?" I told him what I knew and judging by his reactions I could tell it was serious. I began to feel the burning to my hands and face and the smell of smouldering hair was intense. He said we need to get you to the hospital, now! And we sped off through the gates and on to the main road.

Because of the nature of the park with lots of public cars going through it and the dangerous animals within it, all our

Land Rovers and service vehicles had sirens in order to get to an incident through the park traffic. They were not meant to be used on the public highway. However, the boss decided that this was definitely required for this event and so he put the siren on and off we sped to the hospital in Ascot. The journey was only about 10 minutes but as the pain started to take hold it felt like an hour or two. All the time the skin is burning and getting hotter and hotter. We make it to the hospital where I am met by the doctors who rush me through to a cubicle. I am given morphine to help with the pain, which it didn't. The pain just got worse with every minute. They covered my face in cream, put cream all over my hands and then put both hands in plastic bags. They gave me a tub of cream then, remarkably and without any explanation, they sent me home.

The boss drives me home and helps me in to the house. He explained to my mother what had happened and then left. Well. The pain is getting intense by now. I can honestly say that I have never been in so much pain in all my life. It was so bad that I genuinely wanted to cut off my hands to make it stop. My Mum was so concerned that she ordered a taxi and took me off to another hospital in Wexham. I am immediately admitted and the staff sort me out for a ward. Once they dealt with the pain they called a plastic surgeon to take a look at my injuries. The entire right side of my face was burnt with most of my hair singed off. The backs of both my hands were badly burnt and they were my main concern. I had a burn impression of my watch on my wrist from the heat of the metal and a cross burnt on to my chest from a small crucifix I was wearing at the time. The doctors told me that if I hadn't have closed my eyes and mouth at the time of the blast I would have been blinded and my throat could have been so badly burned that I would not have spoken again. If there was any luck involved then I guess this was it. I remained in hospital for the next 28 days while allowing my skin to fall off and recover. The skin would peel and turn black before finally starting to heal. It was pretty horrific. Many of the staff came to visit me and I could tell by their reactions that I looked bad. The hospital staff wouldn't let me use a mirror for fear I would freak out. I am thank full to them for this as I would have been even more paranoid than I already was. The lad who put the petrol on the burner in the first place came to see me. As he walked in to the ward he took one look at me and started to cry. He was so shocked at the consequences of his actions and so apologetic that I couldn't be angry at him. We both made mistakes and his remorse was punishment enough. An investigation was carried out and he accepted his disciplinary and we left it at that. He would have lost his position all together but I didn't want that to happen. We remained friends for the rest of our time at the park. I didn't let him set up the incinerator ever again!

It took three months for me to recover enough to go back to work. The support I received from my family, friends and the Safari Park was second to none.

I often reminisce about the time I was blown up by a Wallaby. The second near death experience of my career, so far. And by the way, don't ever use petrol to light a fire!... Ever!

By now Liam is pretty dumbstruck.

CHAPTER 5

Two sugars please

Let's take a break from trying to kill me off shall we.

The waitress in the restaurant comes over to tell us our dessert is ready. I've been looking forward to this for a while as I do love a good carvery. Liam had ordered fish and chips and we take a short break from the interview while we eat.

A few minutes later we get going again. "It's not all near death when working with animals" I tell Liam. "There's a lot of fun too". As we're sipping our drinks it reminds me of the time when we used to make cups of tea for the Elephants in winter. Nothing better to warm you up on a cold winters day. Liam is quite surprised. "Really!" he says. I laughed. Possibly not the best drink to give an Elephant but they loved it and it doesn't harm them. A nice occasional treat for them. The only difference is, rather than a cup we used a bucket. Several litres of warm water, a couple of dozen tea bags, no milk or sugar and stir well. Remove the tea bags and serve. Good idea I thought. I'll have one myself. Two sugars for me please.

We would sit with the Elephants and have a nice tea break together. They loved it, as did I. Liam laughs. "That's brilliant" he remarks.

That's not the only quirky thing we used to do. At lunch time we used to have access to the canteen for hot meals. We could either sit in and eat or take it away and eat at our respective areas. On this particular day I am assisting up at the Rhino house when a keeper comes round with our lunch delivery. A nice warm plate of roast beef and potatoes with gravy. Lush. The only problem is, our Rhino house didn't have a staff area to sit and eat and to go to a staff area would mean walking through the park with a plate of dinner getting cold. But I had a solution.

The Rhino house was a round building mainly consisting of the animals indoor quarters that was circumnavigated by the staff service corridor. This corridor was raised so you looked down in to the Rhino pen. If the Rhino was in then they would often lean against the wall to rest which meant their back was at keepers waist level with a hand rail to stop us falling in. On this occasion one of the girls was in the house sheltering from the chill outside. Dinner in hand and no table to eat from I turned to my colleague and said, "I have found a solution to the lack of a table," I turned to the Rhino and placed my plate on her back. Don't worry, the plate was not hot. My food was pretty cold by now. The Rhino were used to us stroking and brushing them and were desensitised to touch. With the plate balanced on her back I took a couple of mouthfuls before lifting it off again and sitting on the floor to eat from my lap. I wasn't about to lose my lunch for anyone. I laughed with my mate and said to him, "In years to come I can officially say that I have eaten my dinner from a Rhino's back." And years later, here I am telling the tale. No Rhinos were harmed in the eating of any lunches, although I did have a cold meal.

Liam laughs out loud, "Thats crazy. You've had some amazing experiences". I have to agree. Thinking back over the years I have had some incredible experiences. Working with such incredible animals, seeing special events like rare births such as Tiger or Rhino, and also meeting many famous people and looking after them during their visits. Even Royalty. I have been privileged to escort several members of the Royal family both from the UK and from abroad. This reminds me of one particular event.

We were expecting a Royal visit from an international Royal family. For obvious reasons I cannot name who or where from but I can say he was a King. The Safari Park was often visited by Royalty and used for television due to its location, and Windsor Castle was our next door neighbour. Sometimes high status visitors who had been visiting the Castle would come and visit us. Prior to the Kings visit his entourage would travel ahead of him in order to ensure his security was in place. Two heavily armoured vehicles pulled up at the gate where I was stationed and six huge burley men got out who were all armed! Now because of the nature of the animals all around us, we would have rifles and shotguns to hand in the unlikely event of an emergency. So because of this we were also seen as a potential threat to the visiting King. The armed guards would then stay with me for the entire duration of the Kings visit to ensure that I did not have any desires to assassinate him. Although a nervy experience to have an armed escort it was also very interesting and quite a friendly affair. I got to meet dozens of high status people that you would never normally meet. Prince Charles brought Princes William and Harry round when they were children and they all had a go on the play areas. Sarah Ferguson brought her children too, to name drop just a couple.

Windsor Safari Park was situated within Windsor Great Park which is the back garden of Windsor Castle. We had special permission from the Castle to go in to the woods behind us and collect fresh browse for our Elephants. This we did every couple of days throughout the summer. On one particular day the staff were collecting branches when three people on horses came towards them. They stopped work so as not to spook the horses and stepped to one side to allow them to pass. "Good morning" One of the riders said. "Morning" they replied and looked up. To their shock the person riding the middle horse was the Queen. She was flanked by two security guards. They quickly added "ma'am" to their comment and nodded. She rode off through the woods and the guys carried on with their branching. You don't get that every day on your walk in the woods! So yes, we had some amazing experiences during our time there. She never invited us round for tea though.

While I was at Windsor I had the opportunity to tick off two of my all time top bucket list events. To meet Sir David Attenborough, which i'll mention later, and to go to Africa on safari. Myself and two of my friends and colleagues saved up for around 18 months, and finally we had the chance to go. We spent 12 nights travelling around Nairobi, Mombasa, Tsavo, Masai Mara, Shimbala and several other destinations.

We saw Lions, Rhino, Giraffe, Leopard, Buffalo and so many more iconic species in their natural habitat. It was incredible. We saw Equatorial snow on Mount Kilimanjaro and Mount Kenya. We drove through the area where Joy Adamson had her Leopard rehabilitation ranch and where George Adamson kept his Lions. Famous for 'Elsa' and the 'Born Free' movie as well as their rehabilitation and release of Lions back to the wild. We almost walked in to the jaws of an alligator on our way back to our camp. It was dark and we heard a huge crashing sound right in front of us, then a big splash. The camp guard shone his torch towards the sound just in time to see the Alligator swim off. The guard told us we were very lucky. Not just to see it, but that he didn't attack us! The whole trip was a truly inspiring, wild experience. To get close to the wild counterparts of the animals I cared for at home was truly magical. Seeing new creatures I never thought I would ever see in their native habitat and the natural beauty all around me was something I shall never forget. Nor shall I forget the heat. Often over 40 degrees it was so very different to the weather in the UK. It also made for amazing thunderstorms.

I was immensely lucky to go again a few years later with my then partner. We travelled a different route this time and we were lucky enough to cross the border into Tanzania. We also saw a Leopard up very close. So close in fact that it almost brushed our vehicle. On one occasion a pair of Lions decided to use the shade of our truck to have a rest. They were so close we could have touched them. It was such a privilege. We also saw a Black Rhino in an area that had not seen them for many years. It was thought that they no longer inhabited that area any more. We were the first to spot one in

15 years. Our driver was delighted. As were we. The sighting was later reported to the local authority and recorded as an official, verified sighting. How amazing to be part of that.

We also stayed at 'Treetops' in Aberdare National Park, Kenya where, then Princess Elizabeth, was staying when her father, King George VI died in February 1952. Our room was next to the one she used. We weren't there at the same time mind!

It was one of the best holidays I have ever had. Truly a happy memory for me.

'Treetops'
Picture: © Colin Northcott

Lions in the shade of our vehicle.
Picture: © Colin Northcott.

CHAPTER 6

Media mayhem

Liam: "So meeting all these famous people you must have a few good memories of that?" I reply with a definite yes.

Windsor Safari Park was close to London so it was only a short journey to get there for any potential television or film company. It was also once owned by Granada Television so there were a lot of connections. Pinewood studios and Bray studios were just up the road and the park was often used as a set for several films such as 'The Omen' and 'Mutiny on the Buses' as well as many TV shows like 'Wildlife on One' and several series of 'The Really Wild Show' hosted by Terry Nutkins and Chris Packham. Terry was also a Director of the Safari Park so he would use the park as a filming venue. We didn't really see much of him as he was always away filming, but when he was around he was always polite and informative and a really interesting man to talk to. Having watched him as a child on 'Animal Magic' alongside the great Johnny Morris I couldn't believe that I was now working with him.

A notable show for me was 'Treasure Hunt' starring Annabel Croft. A retired British tennis professional who had taken over the role made famous by Anneka Rice. She would fly around the country solving map location clues guided by contestants in a studio. This was to be my first game show experience. The helicopter landed in the main car park and Annabel leaps out and heads straight for me. For this section of the show the clue was hidden by us according to the previous clue and Annabel had to work out where we had placed it. We had put it up a tree in the Lion enclosure which had 20 plus Lions in, so good luck with that Annabel.

She ran over to me and asked me if I was the Lion keeper. I replied that I was and then ushered her, the cameraman and the sound man into a mobile cage that would take them in to the lions den. That way we could go in to the Lion enclosure without being eaten, or so we hoped. We proceeded to be driven by one of the carnivore keepers to the Lions but on the way we had to go through the Tiger enclosure as it was a one way system. We passed through the large electric gates and were immediately surrounded by Tigers. One of them leaped up on to the cage roof which is covered in steel mesh. Annabel screamed into her microphone "It's on top of the cage, it's on top of the cage!" I couldn't help but laugh. I did this task twice a day, every day so it was normal for me. But to Annabel it was an amazing, and quite a scary experience. She composed herself to keep up her commentary to the studio, not forgetting we have two of the camera crew in with us. We moved away from the Tigers and headed on into the Lion enclosure. Once again we were quickly surrounded by a dozen Lions who all start to claw and climb the cage. At the same time she spots the clue in the tree. Not too difficult as it was bright pink. Annabel then started to panic, "I don't have to get out do I?" The studio contestants shout back with a resounding "NO". I then tap her on the shoulder and offer her a litter picking stick to reach out and grab the clue, which she does quickly and shouts "Stop the clock I have the clue". As the clock is stopped we can now relax and head back to the helicopter and normality was once more upon us. I had a great time filming this and the episode can probably still be found on YouTube if you search hard enough. Don't laugh at my hair cut though eh. After all, it was the 80's.

Liam likes this one as he is a bit of a media buff himself. "There's plenty more where that came from mate" I told him. "What else did you get involved with then?" He asked. "Well, there was the time when Ulrika Jonsson offered me a lift home" I said. "Whaaat!" Liam exclaimed. "You have to tell me about that"

So, bare with me on this. There was a popular TV show called 'You bet' hosted by Bruce Forsyth and later by Mathew Kelly. The show consisted of challenges by members of the public that were backed by celebrities. If the challenger failed his bet then the celebrity who backed them had to do a forfeit. Ulrika Jonsson's challenger had failed his task so Ulrika had to do a forfeit set by the studio. On this occasion the forfeit was to feed the Lions. If you ask me I don't see that as a forfeit but more like an exciting bonus, but that's what the studio gave her. So she comes up to the Safari Park and is escorted to the Lion enclosure where I was waiting to greet her. I run through the safety aspects and off we set to feed the Lions. We spent about an hour filming the feed at various different angles. We finish the task and head back to the safety of the gate. We all pack up and we are just about to set off when Ulrika comes over and say's, "I understand you have come in on your day off for the filming?" I said, "Yes, it's no problem. I have really enjoyed the day" Ulrika then looked at me and said, "Would you like a lift home, there's plenty of room in the car?" Now I only lived about a mile from the park so I could leave my car behind and get a lift from Ulrika Jonsson to my home. This would have gained me a million kudos points and probably I could get her autograph. Being seen by the neighbours and making them jealous, then walking back to the park the following day and picked up my car, would have an amazing tale to tell for the rest of my life. So in answer to Ulrika's question of would I like a lift home I said, "No thank you. I have my car here" .... What was I thinking? The offer of a lifetime from a very glamorous, famous celebrity that was every boys pin-up idol and I turned her down. Sure, I do have a tale to tell for the rest of my life, but not the outcome it should have been. Yes, I have regretted it ever since. My colleagues all thought I was an idiot too. I guess my shy personality got the better of me.

Armoured Land Rover with the big cat feeding cage.
Picture: © Colin Northcott.

Liam shakes his head in dis-belief. "I know. I'm an idiot" I muttered. Thank you to Ulrika for the offer though. I hope she reads this!

"Wow man" Liam said, "That's incredible. Anything else?" "Loads" I said. There was the time when we had been requested to take a Lion cub to the BBC television centre for a piece on 'Going Live' with Philip Schofield and Sarah Green. We trundled off to London and got special permission to pull in to the 'inner circle' of television centre. We put the as yet unnamed twelve week old cub on a lead and started to walk in to the building. By the way, the cub had been rejected by it's mother so was being hand reared by staff and was very amenable. Not something we do nowadays but back in the 80's and 90's it was fairly normal. Anyway, we are walking through the corridors getting a bit star struck at all the famous portraits on the walls. Stars of the day would see us and rather than me getting flustered at meeting a celeb, they were getting flustered at meeting a Lion. The tables had turned and we were now the celebrities. Another keeper, nicknamed 'Ragso' was the main handler and I had tagged along as his assistant so he got to be on the main show live with the cub. I did get to meet Philip and Sarah in the green room prior to the show though. I don't think they would remember me though. They were too busy getting cuddles from the Cat. All great memories that I have never forgotten and with many more to come throughout my career. Not least of which was meeting the legendary Sir David Attenborough.

Sir David would come to Windsor to film for shows such as 'Wildlife on One' and 'Wildlife on Two' among several others that he was involved with. Even though I wasn't directly involved with filming with him I have been immensely lucky to meet him a few times throughout my career and he has been kind enough to sign some books and pictures for me. He was an extremely nice person and he had such an incredible influence on me. "What an honour to meet such an iconic figure" Liam tells me. He is completely right of course.

There was one more interesting event that I attended that made me sweat a bit. Liam gets excited. "Go on, tell me" he says, smiling. Terry Nutkins had been invited to host an event for about 500 children. I can't recall where it was but it was not far from the park. He decided, in his wisdom, to bring a special guest with him. That guest was to be one of our adult Camels. I can't remember it's name. My memory isn't what it used to be. The Camel wasn't fully trained but it was fairly friendly and handleable. So off we go with the Camel in tow. We used a horse box to get to the event. We arrive at the venue and myself and keeper Ragso are rather concerned. The venue was actually a sports hall with a slippery polished floor and an echo to deafen you. We got to the door and waited for our cue to walk in. Terry asks the children to keep quiet and then he introduces us. We walk in with the huge Camel on a double lead. Myself and Ragso stand either side of her head. Then Terry did something that really put the chills on us. He asked the crowd of 500 kids if any of them would like to stroke the Camel. Bare in mind this animal had never been in a building with so many people before. All 500 children with one huge crescendo started screaming and waving frantically to get to stroke the Camel. We both braced ourselves for the impending stampede of kids and a Camel that was about to make a bucking bronco look like a walk in the park. However, to our extreme surprise, and complete relief, the Camel hardly flinched. Terry quickly calmed the crowd and invited just a handful of kids to stroke the Camel. When they had done we turned tail and made a hasty exit, and chalked it down to a favourable win and a lucky escape on our part. We had avoided a potential disaster and Terry was again a hero to 500 kids. Liam, still smiling says, "I love it." It's a great story, now, but it could have been another near death experience at the time! One angry Camel rampaging around a sports hall filled with 500 panicking children would have been a newsworthy event for all the wrong reasons.

Something else that might interest you. London bridge was sold to a wealthy American in 1967 and dismantled for shipping to Lake Havasu in Arizona. The Granite blocks that were left behind were snapped up by Windsor Safari Park and used for landscaping around the enclosures. Most were used for the Baboons and the Lions. They featured in several films including 'Mutiny on the Buses' filmed in 1972. Liam likes this little factoid. Nice and quirky that not a lot of people know about.

Photo from the film, 'Mutiny on the Buses'
Blocks from London bridge can be seen on the left.
Picture: 'Windsor Safari Park staff 1988-1992
photo's and memories'

More London bridge blocks in the
Lion enclosure. Picture: © Colin Northcott.

I have been immensely lucky throughout my career to have met so many famous people and to get involved with making some iconic television and films. I have rubbed shoulders with pop stars such as Rick Astley who, incidentally, appeared to be terrified when we plonked a Lion cub in his arms for a photograph by the local newspaper, and several members of multiple Royal families from all around World. I am truly grateful to Windsor Safari Park for giving me that first break in to the industry and left me with so many happy memories. True, I have had some narrow escapes, but with great support I have come through them all.

I have had loads of fun too...

A film crew at Windsor Safari Park. Circa 1991
Picture: © Colin Northcott.

CHAPTER 7

Up to mischief

Liam: "You must have had some good fun during your time at Windsor?" "Oh yes." I replied. "We had some great laughs, sometimes at the expense of others, but all taken in good spirits"

No animals or people were harmed in the making of the following antics.

A few pranks spring to mind when Liam asked me about it. We had a work experience lad join us. He was a nice lad and we all got on well together, but he was a bit gullible. Something we tended to play on a wee bit!

For the purposes of the story I shall call him Jack. (Not his real name). Jack was assigned to assist at the Elephant house for the day. We had seven African Elephants of various ages. They would be in the house overnight so, as you can imagine, they make a pretty big mess. I have no idea why we had it, but we had an old upright vacuum in the store room. "Jack," we shouted. "Can you give the Elephant house a clean please?" We asked him, and we gave him the upright cleaner and he looked at it a bit perplexed. Without a word he went in to the building, plugged in the extension lead from the staff room and set off vacuuming the floor. Straw, wee, very large poo's all over and he didn't bat an eyelid. He just turned on the cleaner and set to work. We are in the staff area laughing our heads off in disbelief. After only a few moments the cleaner stops and he walks back in to where we are stood. He say's "the bloody thing keeps getting blocked with straw, it'll take ages!" Desperately holding back the laughs we told him, "Keep going, you'll get it done soon enough. Don't worry." To our amazement he turns round and goes back in to the house and starts again. We are in stitches and cannot believe he is carrying on. Eventually we decided to put him out of his misery and stopped him. He saw the funny side and laughed with us about it. We threw the vacuum cleaner away as it was pretty ripe by now!

On another occasion we were talking about our injuries, as you do, comparing scars and bruises gained from working with animals. Jack was with us and I decided to spin him a tale. As a bit of background to this I used to be a smoker, horrible habit that I have kicked many years ago now. Anyway, I used to smoke tobacco and I kept it in a tin that I carried in the leg pocket of my cargo trousers. I started to tell Jack that the boss once got really mad at me while he was driving a mechanical digger. He swung the bucket around and it ripped my leg clean off! Jack is a bit sceptical at this but I had an ace up my sleeve. I could see he wasn't necessarily biting so I had to prove it. "It's true, I have a metal leg" I told him. To prove it I started knocking my tobacco tin while it was in my leg pocket with my hand which gave a handy metallic sound. "See, a metal leg" I said.

He was now convinced and exclaimed, "Oh my god, I didn't know!" "Yeah," I said. "I don't tell everyone as the boss gets embarrassed". Jack is hooked and I take it a little further. "He even knocked off the head of another keeper too!" Jack's jaw drops and he asks, "What, clean off?" I can't help laughing at this point. I didn't think he would believe any of this but he did. At least until I laughed. He twigged and started laughing himself. "You idiots" he said.

Just to clarify. The boss has a license for driving a mechanical digger and did not knock anyone's head off. He also did not chop my leg off and doesn't know about these stories. Unless he is now reading this! Jack was a good lad and he always liked our jokes and tales.

We also told him that the word 'gullible' was the only word in the english language that was not included in the dictionary. He came back to us the following day with a gleeful smile on his face. "I checked that word you told me about, and it is in the dictionary!" He was so happy that he had got one back on us. We left it at that. After his term with us he went back to college and we never heard any more about him. Pranks aside he really enjoyed his time with us and I wish him luck in whatever he is doing now.

There was one story that I have to tell you about that scared me, but was also the funniest thing I had seen in a long time.

My section boss, 'Gunner,' was always a joker and he hatched a plan to have a laugh at the bosses expense. He had an old TV remote control that was about the same size and shape of our two-way radios. These radios were very expensive and we would get in to a lot of trouble if we misused or damaged them. This was one of the bosses pet hates. Gunner said to me "I'm going to wind up the Curator. Watch this." He proceeded to take a bit of plastic that resembled a radio antenna and taped it to the side of the remote control. From a distance it could be mistaken for the two-way. He then got on his real radio and called the boss. "Can you pop down to the Lion enclosure, I need to see you about something." I'm totally intrigued now and can't wait to see what he has planned. In the distance the boss is coming through the Lion enclosure towards us. This is Gunners cue. He starts to make a show of using the two-way with the makeshift remote. He pretends to get agitated with it as if it isn't working properly, so he shakes it and bashes it against his hand as if to try and get it working. All the time he is making sure the boss can see him. Gunner knows that his abuse of the 'radio' will cause the fur to fly. I can see what he is doing now and, knowing the boss is going to be angry at the apparent abuse of the radio, I begin to get a bit nervous at the inevitable shouting match heading this way. The boss pulls in through the gate and he is obviously furious. The car stops and out he gets. It's at this point Gunner shouts, "These bloody radios never bloody work properly!" Then he slams it to the floor smashing it in to dozens of pieces. I can't believe what's happening, and nor can the boss. He immediately goes in to rage and he shouts at Gunner. "What the bloody hell do you think you're playing at?" He rages and goes a nasty shade of red. Gunner, as calm as you like, picks up the keypad part of the remote and starts tapping the buttons. "Bloody thing! I can't get BBC2," and then he starts to smile. I am pretty scared by this because I have no idea how the boss is going to react. The boss has now twigged it's a prank and say's "You bloody idiot. You're going to give me bloody stomach ulcers doing things like that!" he exclaims, and starts laughing. I breath a sigh of relief and I also start laughing. No way could I have got away with a prank like that. It remains one of my favourite moments. Even if it did scare me a bit too!

"That's really funny, I would love to have seen that" say's Liam. "We did loads of things like that" I replied. If you came down to the gate to get your lunch out of your bag it was not uncommon for your bag to be missing. I often found mine half way up a tree between the Lion enclosure and the Tigers. Sometimes you'd find your boots up there too! Banter was important to us and it bonded us together. Something that is very important when you're working with such dangerous animals. We never did anything to hurt anyone. Embarrass them, yes, but never hurt.

There's no denying that we had a fabulous time at Windsor and those funny moments kept you sane in the melee of working in such an environment. They kept us going during the long hours and days and working through all the bank holidays.

Oh, I mustn't forget the time when a Tank went off the main road and drove straight through the Lion fence. "What!" Liam gasped. There were several army barracks around Windsor and their vehicles would often drive past the Safari Park. On this occasion an armoured personal carrier must have swerved for some reason and ended up crashing through the perimeter fence and coming to rest against our main Lion fence. A huge shock for both us, the Lions and the crew of the carrier. No one was injured apart from the pride of the driver. The Lions took an interest but we soon cleared them away from the scene.

"Sounds like you had an amazing relationship with everyone. It must have been a great place" Said Liam. He was dead right.

Chapter 8

Memories and melt down

As I am chatting to Liam, in the back of my mind I keep getting miniature flash backs of things that happened during my time at Windsor. "I'm reminded of a lot of little things that make me smile" I told him. Liam say's, "Go on, what sort of thing do you remember?"

Little oddments, like the time when a construction worker jumped from a build behind the Lion house only to have the ground give way from under his feet with a pretty revolting result! We were having a new station built as a stop for our land train to take visitors around the enclosures. The idea was that we could reduce the number of cars in the enclosures and also provide an opportunity for foot visitors to gain access to the animals. The single story building was at the framing stage and a worker was sitting on the beam when another colleague removed his ladder for a prank. The guy stuck on the beam called out for the ladder to be put back, however, his colleagues told him to jump, as it was only a few feet. The guy looked down and pushed off and landed cleanly, until… Without warning, the ground caved in and he fell in to the hole. He stood up unhurt but a putrid stench suddenly emitted from below.

He looked down to discover that he had fallen in to the carcass of a Camel that had been buried there a year or so previous. He was covered in putrid rotting remains and had to get showered off quick smart.

"That's horrific!" said Liam. "I know, right. But funny all the same," I laughed. I should point out that pre-1980's there were no regulations on burying dead stock and this was common practice. Nowadays of course it is not allowed and they have to be taken away for incineration.

I also recalled the time when we would go out in to the Lion enclosure to strim the ditches to keep them tidy. Nothing unusual about that you may think. Well, in this case it was. The Lions were still out! Liam is gobsmacked. "How did you manage that without being eaten?" he exclaimed! We were always protected by other staff in their Land Rovers who would position themselves between the Lions and the person using the cutters. They also carried firearms just in case. Still not the best way of doing things, but back in the day nothing was straight forward. We had to jump out of our vehicles in the Lion or Tiger enclosures occasionally to tow a customers car that may have broken down, or to pick up something dropped from a vehicle. The animals were used to us being on foot around them. Don't get me wrong, we weren't walking around the park amongst the animals all day, and these events were few and far between. And we never got too close to the animals both for our security and to not alarm the animals. Once again, I stress that this practice is not recommended and rarely continues in wildlife parks today who follow the health and safety guidance.

We did have an old Lion called 'Lordy' who was a lovely old boy. He was about 20+ years old during my time working there. He occasionally required medication to help with his arthritis, but he was very slow and reluctant to come in to the house for it. Sedation at his age was dangerous and we avoided it unless it was vital. So in order for me to give him his medication I used to wait until I saw him walking along, then I would drive right up beside him. He was used to us being in such close quarters when we would help him get around to the house. As I'm now alongside him I would lean out with the syringe and give him a quick injection into his back end. He had no idea what I was doing and we would get the job done without him being stressed and drive away.

One of my favourite stories was when one day our resident falconer came down to the enclosure. He asked us if we had seen his falcon that had absconded from the birds of prey show. All the birds wore tracking devices for just such an event and he had traced it back to the Lion enclosure. We spotted it in a tree just above the sleeping pride. We said that he would have to wait until the Lions were put away before he could go out and search for the bird. He stayed with us to keep an eye of on the monitor and the bird stayed put until the end of the day. As we started to put the Lions inside the bird decided to move. We kept an eye on the Lions and the falconer kept tracking the telemetry. "It's moving towards the house" he said. Thats good, we can get it as soon as the Cats are in. As the last Lion entered the house the bleeps of the tracker stopped at the house. "Weird" he said, "It appears it's coming from inside the Lion house!" We all walked round to the building and sure enough, it took us inside the Lion house. One of the keepers in the house called out. "Oi. This

Lion has a load of feathers in its mouth!" With horror it turned out that one of the Lions had caught and eaten the bird swallowing the telemetry for good measure. We had been tracking the Lion all afternoon! We didn't bother retrieving the device at a later date, if you get my meaning. Pew!

I also heard a story of when the road subsided in the Brown Bear, Black Bear and Wolf enclosure. We had the mix exhibit towards the exit of the main drive through. Just before the large exit gates there was a fairly new section of tarmac. It turns out that many years ago a Killer Whale, that had passed away, was buried in that spot. Over time, as the carcass rotted away, the road began to sink. I wouldn't have been surprised if the animals hadn't had a dig about the area too in search of the rotting corpse beneath their feet! The road had sunk extensively so it had to be replaced. I personally don't know how true this was but that's what the keepers told me and, knowing all the other antics that had happened, it didn't surprise me.

For all the fun and frolics that went on it would all come to an end, breaking the hearts of every single employee who worked there. Out of the blue we were told that the park had gone in to administration and, unless a buyer was found quickly, the park would be closed for good. The shock was immense. We turned up for work the following day to be greeted by hundreds of press and TV crews from around the world covering the story of the closure. They say all good things come to an end. It did in this case.

The receivers did a wonderful job in looking after us and the animals. It appeared that the owners of the Safari Park also owned tourist attractions in Europe and a props supply company for film and TV. These concerns were struggling in the depression of the early 90's but the Safari Park was actually doing well. It was my understanding that they would use the profits of the park to bolster the losses of the other companies until eventually the mother company finally collapsed taking Windsor Safari Park with it. A complete disaster for so many people and animals. Stories in the press were of total doom and gloom. Some stating that over 600 animals would have to be put to sleep. The receivers worked hard to prevent this with many bids from all over the world trying to buy up the park. Eventually a deal was made to the highest bidder. The new owners of the land was to be 'Legoland'. The only proviso was that the animals had to be cleared from the site and we had one year to do it. A terrific blow to us all. But the deal was struck and so we started the daunting task of finding homes for all the creatures.

Over the following twelve months homes were found for every single animal, including the wild Terrapins that lived in the boating lake. They were dispersed all over the world. The Lions were sent to West Midland Safari Park and it was fortunate for me that they agreed to take me on to look after them. So my final days at Windsor were upon me. Although I had the security of a new job, and I would be able to stay with the Lions, it was still a gut wrenching blow that the wonderful joy ride that was Windsor Safari Park was over. Although I didn't transport the Lions myself, I was involved in the releasing of them into their new home at the other end. Lots of media were present for the new arrivals to

Kidderminster. It's not every day 19 Lions travel across the country. But for now I have to leave my friends and family and take with me only memories of wonderful times and wonderful people. I am forever grateful to Windsor for the time I had there, and I can honestly say it was the most incredible time of my entire animal career so far.

On my last day at the park before I headed off to start a new role in the Midlands, everyone gathered around to say a last goodbye. What I didn't know at the time was that while I was talking to everyone there were two others filling my car with balloons and wrapping it with clingfilm! I also didn't know that they had other plans for me too. Suddenly, I was grabbed by some of the lads and they bundled me off to the Elephant house. Without warning they attempted to throw me into the Elephant pond. I wasn't having any of that. It was mid February and was pretty chilly out. I made a valiant effort to escape my captors but failed miserably. I admitted defeat and let them do what they planned. However, I hatched a revenge plan of my own. As one of the guys started to push me in to the pond I grabbed his jumper with a vice like grip and took him in with me. Oh my word, that water was absolutely freezing! I was soaked from head to toe. The other guy was only wet to his waist, but at least I dragged him in with me. Once I got back on dry land the cold really hit me. I started shivering and everyone started to wring me out. If only I had left in the summer, I wished. After saying my goodbyes I ran round to my car and was greeted by the sight of my gift wrapped car. I couldn't help but laugh. It must have taken ages to fill the car with balloons and also to completely wrap the outside in clingfilm. Not an easy task. It took ages to unwrap the car which looked like a brown farm sausage and drive it home surrounded by balloons, whilst shivering from being freezing cold. I loved the day but it was also a very sad one for me.

My final day at Windsor Safari Park was over. I loved it there. A very unique place that I shall never ever forget. It will most likely remain unmatched. I still have contact with some of these very special people and we reminisce from time to time.

Liam: "What a laugh and such a sad time too. It must have been really hard to leave there. But you have some happy memories. I can't imagine what it must have been like to have to leave what seems to me to be such an amazing place."

I know. It was very tough, but sadly necessary.

Press begin to gather at the entrance to the park. 1993.
Picture: © Colin Northcott.

Dunked in the Elephant pool.
Picture: © Colin Northcott

Discovering my car was gift wrapped!
Picture: © Colin Northcott.
"Closed" End of an era!

Picture: © Colin Northcott.

Thank you Windsor Safari Park and all who worked there.

And so I start a fresh and I take my pride of 19 Lions, including Floyd and Pixie on to their own new adventure and new beginnings.

Below is a picture of an amazing Lion we called 'Pixie'. He/she was actually a hermaphrodite. An animal having both male and female sex organs or other sexual characteristics. Several veterinary examinations confirmed this after we had concerns over her slow growth rate. I have never seen or heard of another like her in all my career to date. We treated her as female but she was easily as fiery as any male. She was stunted in growth so only half the size of a regular Lion. She also had a partial mane. However, she could definitely hold her own. I never knew of any occasion when another Lion tried to cross her. Pixie was loved by everyone who met her.

'Pixie'
Picture: © Colin Northcott

CHAPTER 9

New Park and new arrivals

I found a small bungalow in Bewdley that I shared with another Windsor keeper, 'Big Al'. So named because he was quite short, obviously! He also came up to the Midlands to look after the Lions. The Safari Park already had Lions but they were contained in an enclosure so the visitors were unable to drive through to see them. The idea of the Windsor Lions was to create a new drive through section. Part of my new job was to assist with the building of the enclosure and then to settle the Lions in. I also had to teach the keepers the art of looking after Lions in close proximity. Luckily for me, the Windsor Lions were already professionals so they were the least of my worries. Eventually the enclosure was ready and it was now a case of collecting the Lions from Windsor and putting them in to their new home. The Deputy Warden drove the lorry down to Windsor where the Lions would be crated and loaded on board. After a two hour drive we would unload the Lion laden crates, put them up to the entrance to their new housing, lock them in place, then lift the hatch to release the Lion. Easy?

The first batch of Lions arrived at West Midlands amongst a hoard of media interest. It's not every day this kind of thing happens so it was understandable. Everything was set up and we started to unload the crates.

One by one they exited their crates and ran straight in to the dens. All ran smoothly. Good job really, especially when you have dozens of TV cameras filming your every move. The last Lion, 'Green Tag,' so named because she had a green tag in her ear when she was younger. She had other ideas. The hatch was opened and she just sat there. She gazed out at the gathering, bared her teeth and growled at us. It must have been unnerving for her after all the upset of the journey and then to see her pride members going through the same ordeal, so I can't blame her. Eventually she decided to make a run for it. But not without leaving her mark and reminding everyone that she was the most powerful beast amongst us. As she stepped out of her crate she turned her head to the framework and took a huge chunk out of it leaving a Lion sized bite hole behind. Caught on film it made it on to the local news programme later that night.

So the Lions were in and it was time to settle in to the new position and make new friends and memories. Another animal that I knew well which made it up to the Midlands was the Hippo, 'Gertie,' and her family. This helped make my transition much easier as I had a head start on a lot of the animals that the keepers needed to learn about, and so, my new job began.

Over time I looked after many more of the animals, including the Tigers, Painted Dogs, Wolves and even got involved with all the hoof stock including Giraffe and Cape Buffalo. Later on I spent a lot of time with the parks

Elephants. There was no shortage of work to be done and we often had work experience and intern students to assist us.

"You'll appreciate this Liam" I said. We had an intern or whatever he was, I lose track. It was a long time ago, about 1997 or thereabouts. Anyway, we had a travelling Dinosaur exhibition visiting us for a few weeks. They were animatronic so appeared very life like. We decided to have some fun with the new lad. We gathered a wheelbarrow, broom and shovel and called him over. "Can you do us a favour and go and clean the Dinosaurs please?" I said, and handed him the equipment. He looked at me as if he was going to say something but I kept a perfect poker face, so he thought I must be serious. He duly collected the barrow and started to walk down to the exhibit. A few yards down the track he stopped. He's twigged, I thought. He walked back to me looking puzzled. "Aren't they dangerous?" He asked. Laughing inside I said, "Nah, you'll be fine, they're very placid." So off he went and disappeared out of sight. A few minutes later we received a radio call from the security guard looking after the exhibit. "Have you just sent a lad down to clean out the Dinosaurs?" he asked. "Yes," Is he doing a good job?" I replied. "We'll make sure he does" came the answer. My Windsor days mischief were still valid at the new park.

It wasn't all pranks and mischief. There was a serious side to all of this work too. Conservation and preservation is high on the agenda for zoos and wildlife parks and West Midlands was no exception. One important job we got involved with was testing out new animal tracking devices for use in Africa. This was in order to study Lion and Rhino behaviour and movements in the wild. When devices are made for such a task they have to be trialed and where better to do this than in a controlled environment with the very animals they were intended for. So the manufacturers came to us. The new satellite tracker was placed on one of our Lions, and also a Rhino. We had to sedate the Lion in order to place the collar then we could leave her to her normal routine. Back in their office the manufacturer of the collar could track the Lion by satellite to ensure the smooth running of the equipment. It was also a trial to make sure that the devices were actually Lion and Rhino proof and to ensure that they would not harm the animals. After a few weeks the collars were removed and the test was deemed a success. The collars were later used on wild animals in Africa and were the pre-curser to todays modern devices used for wild animal study.

Colin and a sedated Lioness in preparation for the tracking collar to be fitted.
Picture: © Colin Northcott

Working with so many animals over the years it's inevitable that they are going to breed. As part of the role of conserving animals breeding is obviously vital, but so is not breeding. Most captive endangered species are controlled by a 'stud book'. Essentially this is a dating agency for animals. The holder of the stud book, each species has its own administrator in charge, will have the family background of most of the individuals within the captive collections. Because the family can be traced for each one of a species they can be matched with the best single potential mate in order to prevent the blood lines from being diluted and ensure a good, healthy gene pool is maintained. This in turn ensures only the fittest and healthiest animals are available for re-wilding should they ever be required. The stud book makes the recommendations to each collection as to where individual animals should go to breed but its down to the collection to arrange the movement of those animals. Wild animal parks are restricted by space so it's important to only breed when there is somewhere for the young to go. This also prevents overcrowding. If you do not wish to breed then contraception is used.

At West Midlands we were in the position to breed so we had several young Lions and Tigers over the years. Now there is nothing more satisfying than successfully breeding your charges. There's nothing more endearing than a baby animal too. Making sure the youngsters are fit and healthy meant that occasionally you had to get hands on with them so at around nine weeks old you would separate them from their mother and give them a health check, sex them, weigh them , give them their first inoculations and generally make sure they were developing well. This would only take a few moments and they would soon be back with their mum. All the time she would be in the next den to oversee the operation. At around twelve weeks you would repeat the operation only this time you would give them their second inoculation and anything else they may require, as well as a microchip for identification. I bet there isn't a keeper in the land that has been able to resist a bit of a cuddle with a baby animal either, and I am no exception.

"I would have loved an opportunity like that. What an experience and a privilege to do what you do," Liam cuts in. And he is right. I am waffling on about my history and almost forget to allow him to get a word in. But that's the whole idea and reason for our conversation. He makes a comment and I rattle on with a memory. Thanks Liam.

Piggy back time. The cubs loved to play.
Picture: © Colin Northcott.

Colin with two Tiger cubs.
Picture: © Colin Northcott.

A quick snap shot and they are back with their mum. Fit and healthy. After 12 weeks they are not handled again unless it is required for health reasons. Of course, having cubs were a big attraction and visitors would love to see them out playing in the enclosures. The media would love it too and we would have an influx of television companies coming in to catch a glimpse of them. Lion, Tiger, Wolf, you name it, they would want to film it. An opportunity to educate and good for business too. Bringing in the public meant more revenue for the park and more money can go towards conservation.

CHAPTER 10

More media attention

Summertime was always a busy period for us. Not just because of the visiting public but it was also the main time of the year when most of the animals gave birth which in turn attracted the most media attention. "What sort of thing did you get?" Liam asks. We had a whole range of stuff.

Apart from the local news coverage of Lion arrivals or endangered species births we also had children's TV shows recording segues for their series or to do an entire show from the animal enclosures. We would often be a guest on the show to discuss what we did and to talk about the animals. A perfect platform to inform the public about conservation.

On one occasion Channel 4's 'Big Breakfast' with Chris Evans and Gaby Roslin was filmed live at the Safari Park. It was an absolute blast. Keith Chegwin also came to film around the park and I escorted him to various points to film. He was very funny and we really enjoyed the day.

Quite often a film crew would use the park to recreate wild scenes for natural history programs. They would dress an enclosure to make it look more authentic to a particular area of the world so they could get controlled footage of an animal reacting. We didn't mind this as it meant that the animal involved got a bit extra to explore in its own enclosure, which is always good for enrichment. Sometimes the accompanying book for that series would credit us and include some photographs of the scenes we created. Our services were required to provide expert advice on the species around the park. It definitely broke any sort of mundane routines we may have had.

Michaela Strachen filming at the Elephant enclosure for the BBC. Picture: © Colin Northcott.

Nickelodean TV in the Emu enclosure in 2004.
Picture: © Colin Northcott.

GMTV in 2004.
Picture: © Colin Northcott.

Of course inevitably we would meet many famous people along the way. Far too many to name, which in itself is pretty amazing. I have already mentioned the great Sir David Attenborough. Truly a highlight of my animal career. However, it also meant some pretty unsociable hours too. The Big Breakfast and GMTV were clearly early starters. Usually going out live they had to be set up and running with plenty of time to sort out any issues before broadcast. That meant being at work sometimes for 5am. As we were open until 6pm it meant that we couldn't go home early that day either. So you have to be prepared to work long hours when required. It was okay though. The perks we got were great and sometimes meeting your heroes, like Sir David, or finding yourself in front of the camera for all the world to see.

The long hours stretched to the animal maintenance too. If they were sick or required attention due to moving to or from another establishment then you had to be there for it. No if's, no buts, the animals need you and it's what you sign up for when you join the industry. At least, that's how I see it. Animal welfare should always come first and although some of my stories may seem a little odd, the animals were always at the top of the care list.

Oh, and you can forget Christmas Day. If you're rota'd in for it then you have to attend. It's just another day to the animals. Hopefully your management has a system in place that makes it fair for all. But, to be honest, working when the park is closed is pretty awesome anyway. You can spend more time with the animals which strengthens the bond. It's all good.

CHAPTER 11

Foot-and-mouth

It's probably evident by now that I may have gone a little off piste. Liam is still with me and we are chatting away. Food long eaten and drinks are still on the go. Our conversation is so much fun and I can't help myself but to keep talking about my history. Liam is captivated, or so he tells me. Good man.

There was an event that really hit me hard during my time at West Mids. Back in February 2001 the UK was struck by Foot-and-Mouth disease. A devastating illness that wiped out over six million Cows, Sheep and other farm animals all over the UK. It was not restricted to just farms either. If you were within a certain distance of a confirmed foot-and-mouth case then your livestock also had to be destroyed. If you were just outside the infection zone then restrictions on animal related movements were put in place. This included staff and deliveries to and from animal areas. Foot-and-mouth was discovered near enough to the park to enforce restrictions upon us. This meant that the park had to close its doors to any visitors indefinitely. That meant no income was being generated but money was still being spent on looking after the animals.

The park set up perimeters and put in place heavy duty foot dips for pedestrian traffic and deep dips for essential vehicle movements, including spraying down the vehicles with disinfectants from top to bottom, concentrating on the tyres, ensuring the vehicles drove through deep littered disinfectant mats.

Foot-and-Mouth check point at the
West Midland Safari Park 2001.
Picture: © Colin Northcott

There was only one way in and out to ensure against mistakes. With the animals we had at the park we had to be extremely cautious. Even feed bags were treated too. The closure went on for months.

Eventually the restrictions were lifted but we still had to take precautions. Foot visitors had to dip their feet and every single vehicle that entered the park was sprayed. Very muddy vehicles, like farm transport, were not allowed on site. Hand wash stations were placed everywhere. It was impossible to enter or exit without being disinfected. Veterinary monitoring of the animals was a daily routine and the slightest sign of any concern caused by an animal was investigated immediately and quarantine style procedures were put in place until we had the all clear.

All this came at a huge financial cost. Paying for all this must have been astronomical. The restriction of movement for everyone meant that visitor numbers were drastically reduced. This went on for the whole summer, which was the parks busiest time. In fact the country wasn't given the all clear until September 2001 and restrictions were not lifted until January 2002. Thankfully no animals at the park were lost to this awful disease.

However, that meant that cuts had to be made. One way of saving funds was to make some staff redundant. And I was one of them. I was called in to the office without warning and told the news. I have never been hit so hard in all my life. It was devastating. I had just lost the job I loved so much through no fault of my own, or the parks doing. At the same time I had just separated from my wife and this blow hit me like a truck to the stomach. Financially I was strapped also. I had a mortgage to pay for and an expensive solicitor to fund too. I know that many people go through these things in their lives but to me, they all came together. In one month I had lost my wife, my car, my home, and to put icing on the cake I had the news that my brother had suffered a heart attack a few days prior. He was okay and doing well but it meant I could not go and see him as he was hundreds of miles away.

Liam: "I am so sorry to hear this mate. All that in just one month. Pretty tough to cope with." "I totally understand why you're not talking about your private life, so to speak". "Thanks. It's not right to tell a tale of those who can't reply and I wouldn't want to say something that they felt they had a different point of view to" I told him. "Fair enough." He said.

So. With that in mind I had a period of time not working at the park. But wait.............

A few short months later I was re-instated. "Thank goodness for that" said Liam. "Absolutely" I said. Back at it and I put that short break behind me.

I would just like to say that I am very grateful to the people who helped me through that period for the financial assistance given by my family and for the work given to me by others. Thank you all.

Right. Back to it. With foot-and-mouth well and truly eradicated and having moved house, but still in Kidderminster, I can get back to some form of normality. At least a Safari Parks type of normality.

A while later I had another heart stopping moment. This time it was instigated by a Tiger called 'Harlem'. As a Safari Park keeper we are in amongst the animals every day. If an animal does anything that is deemed as dangerous then we can move the animal with our vehicles. Never hitting them, but approaching them with enough positivity that the animal moves away. If an animal was stubborn and didn't want to go in the house we could give them some persuasion with the vehicle.

On this occasion the Tiger in question was being particularly stubborn. His enclosure was on a slope and it was damp so I had to use the four wheel drive to approach him. He started to move off but suddenly he doubled back and decided to have a game with me. I'm sideways on to the slope so manoeuvring was pretty difficult. Suddenly he grabbed the back quarter of the car, in this case a Suzuki Vitara. He sank his teeth in to the pillar between the passenger side and the back door and held me fast. I tried to move but he was so strong I just wheel span on the spot. He then tightened his grip which shattered the passenger side window. What was worrying was I still couldn't move and this vehicle was a short wheel base. Knowing the glass was now gone the Tiger then managed to get his front left paw inside. With a thud he hit the toolbox I had inside the back. Now partly inside the cabin he was getting heavier on the suspension which meant I had even less chance of moving. Then he released the grip he had with his mouth in order to get his other leg in the vehicle too. Which unfortunately he did! Closely followed by his head. It's at this point I'm beginning to get a bit concerned that this might be getting pretty serious. By now I was beginning to drift the vehicle slightly because of the weight shift, but he just came with me! He started to swipe at my head and I could feel the wind from his paw as it swung close to my head. I could even smell his meaty breath, which was quite unpleasant.

I'm now leaning forward on to the steering wheel hoping that somehow I would find some grip and get away. The shifting Tiger and my vigorous driving somehow found some traction. I later found out from observers that my wheel had caught on a bone which jolted the vehicle in to some grip. That jolt put the Tiger off balance enough for me to swing the vehicle round and he dropped back out. Free of the tiger I turned the vehicle around and went back to him to drive him in to the house where the keepers put him away to cool off. I drove out of the enclosure and breathed a sigh of relief. The others told me that, from their point of view, I was a goner. They were on the radio calling for immediate assistance. I didn't hear any of those calls as I was a little busy at the time. I chalked it down to another close shave that comes with the territory. If I was a Cat who was good at maths, I think that was life number three gone. Or four if I had included the time when I was sixteen when a collapsed lung did actually kill me. I only survived by the quick work of the hospital.

So four lives down, I continue.......

Three young Tigers at West Midland Safari Park.
Picture: © Colin Northcott

CHAPTER 12

Fire and foul play

Liam: "I can't believe the close calls you've had. It's a pretty dangerous job to be fair." "It has its moments" I reply. You have to remember that all this was many years ago and recent changes in the industry as a whole, prevents anyone from getting in to dangerous situations. However, the animals you work with don't always read the rules and they sometimes do things that require you to think outside the box. Keepers that work in close proximity to animals that can kill you have to make decisions that could potentially save your. Not just for the keeper, but for members of the public and even the animals. The set up of zoos and safari parks now are completely safe as long as you don't do anything stupid to put yourself in danger. So if you're driving through a safari park, don't think it's a good idea to stop and have a picnic in the Lion enclosure or you'll find that the Lions might just have you for their picnic!

Sometimes danger comes from other areas that you might not expect. "What do you mean?" asks Liam.

Well....

West Midland Safari Park is between Kidderminster and Bewdley. The famous Severn Valley Steam Railway runs between Kidderminster and Bridgnorth and the track runs directly along the perimeter of the Safari park as it reaches Bewdley. This makes for some spectacular views of the steam trains as they trundle past the animals. Seeing Elephants against a back drop of steam engines in full puff is pretty awesome, and pretty unique in the UK. However, having steam engines running past your enclosures can have a few issues too. The animals are used to them so the noise and whistles are never an issue. The problem comes when the smoke stack chuffs out hot embers that fall on dry grass. This happens many times a year if you have a particularly dry summer.

Many times I was called upon to attend the perimeter because the grass banks were alight. I must stress that no animals were ever in danger but we couldn't allow a fire to go unchecked. With a large wooded area a Site of Special Scientific Interest, (SSSI) beside us, we didn't want to run the risk of a huge fire. We had special grass fire mats dotted around the site so usually all we had to do was to get to the fire and pad it out with the mats. The railway also had fire watch staff that would attend all along the track too, so between us we always got it sorted. On the rare occasion the fire would get a bit big for us then the local fire service would attend.

The park was ready for this and we maintained a 'fire break' between us and the tracks that we would patrol and upkeep. This also acted as an access road to be able to get fire tenders to the site should it be needed. So not only were we animal keepers, we were fire wardens, first aiders and, in my case, firearms officers too. Multi-talented staff indeed.

It wasn't just the trains that caused fires. Sometimes a customers car would go up too. It's actually more common than you might think. We would have at least five or six car fires throughout the year. Not a good situation if you're in the middle of a Lion or Tiger enclosure. Often caused by cars driving long distances at very low speed and the engine bay overheating causing electrical fires and sometimes fuel fires.

One way of dealing with it would be to evacuate the occupants in to your vehicle then shove the burning car out of the enclosure to a safe area. Cars don't just explode in to a ball of flames like you see in the movies so we always had time to move it. Of course, we all carried fire extinguishers with us so if you could put the fire out safely then we would. If the fire was too much then the fire service would be called. While waiting for their attendance we would clear the area of animals and people to allow safe passage.

I remember one particular car fire we had. It was a Land Rover Discovery and it had stalled in the African enclosure. Staff noticed thick smoke emitting from under the bonnet so immediately took the occupants to safety and called for assistance. We started to clear the road for the fire service to attend. An observant member of staff noticed that the fuel filler cap was different to the usual one fitted to these cars. I looked closer and realised that this particular vehicle was gas powered. This changed everything! If a gas container was to blow it could destroy everything around it and shrapnel from

81

the vehicle could kill anyone close. Immediately we made the cordon bigger. The fire service arrived and, by this time, the front of the vehicle was ablaze. We informed them about the gas canisters and they were a bit shocked. They treated the blaze very differently to the usual car fire by evacuating the entire area and using less crew to tackle the blaze. They also used a foam type substance to dowse the flames. Their swift action meant that the fire was out before the tank exploded. I dread to think what could have come of it should it have blown. I asked one of the fire men what might have happened. He said that the car would have disintegrated and we could have had multiple injuries or even deaths to contend with too. It really woke us up to the potential disasters that we could be facing on a daily basis. It's hard enough to be working around animals that could eat you, let alone vehicles that could barbecue you first!

Car fire at WMSP 2003.
Picture: © Colin Northcott.

That was just one incident that stuck in my mind because of the potential disaster that was thankfully averted. Car fires were fairly common so we became very proficient at dealing with them swiftly so most were fairly uneventful. Not so much for the owners but we also assisted them in the aftermath. We arranged for transport to get them home safely and helped with the recovery of the vehicle.

"Wow. I never thought about the possibility of car fires. Anything else happened while you were there?" Liam asked me. "Yes, it did" I replied.

Outside the parks perimeter was a scout camp for weekend overnight scout groups to earn their badges etc. Unfortunately they suffered a break in and the culprits stole a set of Bows and arrows and decided to loose a few arrows over our fences. I came to work one day and started my animal checks. I arrived at the Wallaby enclosure to find half a dozen arrows scattered around the enclosure. We weren't sure if the people involved intended to fire at the animals but fortunately no animals were harmed. It would have been very dark and the enclosures very large so hitting anything would have been very slim. We informed the Police and the owners of the scout huts and nothing more came of it. But it just highlights that you never know what you're going to find when you go to work in the morning. This was further reinforced on a routine fence inspection.

Every day all our fences would be checked for integrity. You don't want to come to work to find your Tigers wandering around the car park! Part of the routine animal checks involved driving the enclosure perimeters. I am very glad we did because as the Head Warden was driving the fire break alongside the SSSI land he came across a rather large hole in the fence. On further inspection we could see that the fence had been cut. The hole was large enough for some of the smaller animals to get through. Fortunately the animals in that area were various Deer and Antelope species so none of them were man eaters. Except for 'Rambo' the Wapiti, or Elk. During the rutting season he was pretty dangerous and he would chase us all over the enclosure to get to the food. Being so huge, about the size of a Horse and weighing in around 320 kilograms, he could have done some real damage. We took precautions by removing his antlers so when he head butted at us he would miss us by about four feet. Their antlers are huge! He would also try and climb up on to the tractor trailer if we weren't careful. He would give out a high pitched bellowing that could be heard from miles around. He was so impressive. Anyway, I digress. So this hole was pretty big. But not big enough for Rambo to get through. In fact, none of our animals got through it and we swiftly repaired the hole while others informed the Police.

Deer are quite interesting really. If they have been in an enclosed area for many years they learn where their boundaries are and are comfortable with what they do within it. So much so that you can actually remove a section of fence and the Deer won't cross the now wide open line. Happy grazing along it, but not wishing to walk over it. It's not until they discover the fresh grass across the threshold that they start to stick their necks out to eat it, then over time, they find themselves through. This has been proven to me when we removed an entire fence line to allow a herd of Fallow Deer to go through to another area and, although they would graze along it, they would not cross the original fence line for several days.

A few days later whilst on our routine fence checks we discovered another section of cut fence on the same enclosure. Again nothing had escaped but it was becoming clear that we had an issue. Once again the Police were informed but they couldn't do anything without a crime happening at that moment in time. After a third occurrence we decided to hold a night time vigil to see if we could catch the culprits. We made arrangements with the Police and I was to be placed up in one of our high gate towers to get a good view of the perimeter fence. Armed with night vision binoculars I waited for any action. With the phone number of the local Police who were also waiting in other areas, I sat and waited, and waited......... and waited...... Until..... Nothing! Four nights in a row nothing happened. The decision was made to stop the night watches as I was required at the park during the day. Guess what. Yep. On the fifth night they cut the fence again. We couldn't believe it. So we watched again. Night after night but to no avail. When we finally gave up the surveillance we fully expected a recurrence. Fortunately we didn't get one. We never did find out who did it but it was a little coincidental that a local toe rag had been arrested in an unrelated incident at the same time as ours stopped.

No matter how good your facility is you can never account for outside forces.

CHAPTER 13

Vet visits

Don't worry, Liam is still here. Listening intently to my chat. "There's a lot more where all that came from" I joked. "I bet. So what else can you tell me about next?" He asks.

Working over the years with what amounts to thousands of animals, it's inevitable that some of them will become ill. Animals in a captive situation have the best quality medical treatment when sickness befalls them. So much so that for some species their life span has increased by quite a substantial amount. As a result of this these animals become susceptible to illnesses and ailments that their wild counterparts probably would never encounter. In line with this, exotic animal veterinary techniques and knowledge have come on leaps and bounds. I have had the absolute privilege to work with some of the best vets in the country. Now there have been thousands of various procedures over the years, far too many to list. Besides, my memory can't cope with it! So, if I may indulge, I will mention just a few notable occurrences where I have been involved with a few treatments, incidents, whatever you want to call them.

I remember the time when we were locking up at the Wolf enclosure. We noticed one of the Wolves was wriggling on the floor in obvious discomfort. On closer inspection we could see his fur was moving around the shoulder blades. Maggots. The Wolf was fly struck. Fly strike is when an animal has an injury that is open to flesh and, especially in the summer months, flies get on to the wound and lay their eggs. When the eggs hatch the maggots start to eat the flesh of the animal causing intense irritation, and, if not discovered quickly and in a worse case scenario can lead to death. When the animal has a lot of deep fur it is very difficult to spot until, sometimes, it's too late.

Our Wolf was clearly in discomfort and we had to call the vet. In this case it was the late David Taylor who attended. He was a founder member of the International Zoo Veterinary Group. IZVG. Founded in 1976 with Andrew Greenwood. They are now the largest full time freelance zoological veterinary practice in the world. So we were in the best of hands. I particularly remember this visit because when he arrived he was wearing a full black bow tie dinner jacket. We were shocked as it's not the usual attire the vet turns up in. "I'm on my way to a gala dinner" he said. We apologised for diverting him but, ever the professional, he said, "Don't be daft, the animals need help." So we got down to business.

We sedated the Wolf on a fairly light sedative but enough for us to handle him. David cut away the dead and problematic skin. We cleaned out the maggots and ensured there were none hiding elsewhere. We treated the wound and gave him antibiotics, made sure there were no more injuries and revived him. David waited until the Wolf was back on his feet and then made his exit to the celebrity dinner he was guesting at. As he walked away we could see that he had mud down his trousers. I looked at the other staff in attendance with a wary smile. David also noticed and said. "I'm a vet, it goes with the territory. I can change later. Any problems give me a call" He waved and off he went. We never discovered the original cause of the injury but it can come from something as simple as a small cut. Anything that a fly can get to. The Wolf made a full recovery.

Not all illness has a good outcome. We had a troubling event that shook us all to the core. We took a call from the Baboon enclosure to say that they had found two animals had died over night. To have two at once is unusual so this warranted further investigation. We called IZVG and David came out. By the time he arrived we had another Baboon brought over that had also died. This is not good. David started to do a post mortem. He took several samples and packaged them up to send away. The following day even more animals were dying. We couldn't believe it. What the hell was going on! David was spending more and more time at the park to try and get to the bottom of what was happening. No matter the age, old or young, they were dropping like flies! We were devastated. The vets were working like crazy. Sample after sample was taken. If you have been looking after a particular species for many years you can't help gaining a special bond. With some of them they become like friends. Those with special characters would become your best buddies. To see them all dying in front of you for no apparent reason was so heart wrenching. It was horrible for all of us. The late Dr. John Lewis, also from IZVG was also involved in finding out what was happening. John finally diagnosed the cause. Botulism, this is a very rare but life-threatening condition caused by toxins produced by Clostridium botulinum bacteria, which was confirmed after testing by London Zoo. We could finally protect the rest of the troop with a serum brought over from the USA. If my memory serves the final death toll was 42. A devastating number. The cause turned out to be some cooked ham that had found its way in to the Baboons food and mistakenly fed out to the troop. The efforts made by the David, John and the staff were second to none and something I shall never forget. This was the first time I had witnessed a mass loss of life.

But it wasn't to be the last.

'I'm so sorry mate. It must have been horrible to witness such a thing. I can't imagine it." Liam said. "I can see it happening in my mind to this day. Baboons have a way of looking at you straight in the eye, and with a knowing gaze! I never want to go through that again" was my reply. A little choked I carry on.

On another occasion we had a Lion called "CJ" with a pretty serious tooth ache. Now this is going to be interesting I thought. This was a new one to me so early in my career. Once again we called upon the services of IZVG, only this time a specialist dentist was called upon to deal with this case. Only the best will do, so Dr Peter Kertesz was called. He owned a dental practice in Mayfair, London. He was also an exotic animal dentist. I understand he was the first dentist to ever remove an adult Bull Elephant tusk at the root. If he can do that then a Lion tooth is a doddle right?

So the Lion is ready. We took him from the pen, sedated obviously, and place him on a makeshift bed built from straw bales. Peter needs the head to be at a particular angle to get a good go at the tooth. We had nothing to hand and time was of the essence so we improvised. I was a bystander so I jumped in and placed my arm, upright, under the Lions head to raise it enough for Peter to work on. What an amazing experience to be able to watch the procedure. It was fascinating. Although I hadn't anticipated quite how long it was going to take. After what felt like an hour Peter said to me, "Are you okay there, do you need to change arms?" I replied "No thanks. My arm is already numb, you might as well keep going." So he did. Finally the procedure was over and I could get my arm back. But it was so worth it. The Lion was ready to be revived so we all got ready to lift him back into the pen on a stretcher. The sedative reversal was administered and we lifted him up and walked to the door. It was only six feet away. As we stepped in to the pen the Lion decided that this was when he was going to wake up! He shifted his head and growled. Everyone dropped him and ran! Except me. I grabbed a large metal fork designed to fit over a big cats head to hold it down without choking it. I placed it swiftly over his neck and looked up to see everyone else had backed off! I was either brave or stupid to stay with the cat. I'd like to think I was brave. After about 30 seconds, that felt like minutes, the Lion dozed off again and we dragged him back in to the pen and locked him safely away.

Reviving animals always has its risks, as does the sedation. Animals can come round at different rates. Some take hours, some take minutes and some can take seconds. I witnessed an Antelope come round as the injection needle was being removed. I also saw a Wolf come round less than 30 seconds after revival. You always have to be on your guard and only administer the drug at the very end of the procedure when everything else is finished. Doses also vary for each individual according to size, weight, age and fitness so it's never an exact science.

Finally the job was done and no one was hurt. The whole procedure was filmed by the local ITV news station, now Meridian, so if you're any good on a computer you might be able to find it. I'm not so good so I have not found it yet! So good luck.

Other procedures that require veterinary interventions are difficult births. I recall one where a Zebra was struggling to foal. The vet was called and we got to work. It was clear that this was not going to be easy so the vet asked me to run out to the local shop and get some soap flakes. I duly ran out to my car and sped off to the nearest shop. I grabbed every packet of soap flakes they had and the puzzled cashier asked "You have a lot of washing to do eh?" I replied, "not quite. We're helping a Zebra to give birth," and ran out of the store, just catching a glimpse at her jaw dropping with disbelief.

I arrived back at the Zebra house where everyone was waiting. The vet said, "Who has the skinniest arms?" To which everyone turned and looked at me. Puzzled, I said, "Me I guess. Why?". "Take your shirt off and soap up. I need you to put your arm up here alongside mine and help me move the foal" He said. Slightly anxious I did as he asked and took off my top and soaped my arms up. He held my hand in a closed point and steered me up through the animals vulva to the head of the unborn foal. "As I pull the legs you need to steer the head around" He told me. I have never done anything like this before so I was pretty nervous by now, but I had a large audience and this animals life depended on us, so without hesitation I did as I was told. It was a very strange sensation. Warm and slimy and I could feel pulses of life. As my arm reached beyond my elbow I could feel some movement. I found the head and started to push and twist it around. I glanced round to see three other people gently pulling on the foals legs using a rope which had now come through. Slowly but surely the foal was finally born. However, to everyones regret, she was dead. The birth was a breach and as the head was twisted in the womb it could not be born correctly hence the intervention. We also noticed that, by a freak of nature, rather than two normal front legs, she had two back legs! Her actual back legs were normal, so essentially she was born with four back legs. Something I have never come across again and hopefully never will. That's nature for you I guess. It throws a few surprises at you from time to time.

Over the years I have witnessed many births, and seen many deaths. There is little more satisfying than successfully breeding an endangered animal. I have assisted with Lion births, Tigers, Painted Dogs and Giraffe to name just a small few. Most animals give birth at night when it's dark and quiet and the mother won't be disturbed. When this happens the best way to monitor the birth is via night vision CCTV. I have been able to record Tigers, Tapir and Painted Dogs through the birthing process. Stayed up all night to monitor to ensure nothing goes wrong. It's a real wonder of nature to witness such a thing.

One day one of our Giraffe was going in to labour. This was in the middle of the day so it was pretty unusual. All we could do was to watch and hope it went well. Giraffe give birth standing up so there was no way we could assist safely even if she was in trouble. She spends her time pacing the pen and suddenly the legs appear. After a few moments the head then the body and the rest of it flops to the floor. Because they give birth standing, the fall is quite long, about six foot. But by the time the back legs give way from the mother the head and front legs are already closer to the floor so it isn't as dramatic as you may think. Baby out and mother relaxing we make sure all is well and we leave them to bond and get to know each other. A wonderful thing to see and I will never tire of witnessing. Even for a seasoned keeper it is still a rare thing to witness.

Front legs first before the head appears as if
to 'dive' to the ground. Picture: © Colin Northcott.

A beautiful baby boy.
Picture © Colin Northcott.

Some of the less happy events are when you lose an animal in your care. Death is always a tough one for a keeper. We are all used to it and we expect it, but it never really gets easy. When an animal does die we invariably do an autopsy on it to find out exactly why it has happened. If it's old age then that comes to us all eh. If it is unexpected then it needs to be investigated so you can hopefully prevent it from happening again. Even if you know why the animal died, you can always discover things that you may not have known had you not performed the post mortem. So it's a vital part of the job. Obviously it's up to a qualified vet to do this, but we often get involved too. The knowledge a keeper has of its charges can be very useful to a vet in order to understand certain aspects of the animals in question. Why an animal may have a historical injury or previous illness that the vet may not know about.

There were three post mortem's that I assisted with that have stuck in my mind. The Baboons were particularly bad as they have such human like qualities that are quite spooky to deal with. Another was a Cheetah named "Safari" that had passed away. I can't recall if it was John Lewis or David Taylor from IZVG, but one of them came to do the autopsy. Nothing unusual about the scenario, but it was the interesting fact that they gave me whilst watching what was going on that has always stuck in my mind. The Cheetah had been completely opened up. The intestines, heart, lungs were all removed and the vet was going through the various organs looking for unusual signs. While he was doing this I was at the head. It's not every day that you can get so close to these animals without being eaten, so I was getting hands on with it. I was exploring around the head when the vet

95

shouted "STOP!" This made me jump and I stepped back. I was about to feel the teeth and I guess this wasn't a good idea. The vet said, "You should never put your fingers in the mouth, it'll bite you" I laughed and said, "You had me fooled for a second." He replied with, "I'm not joking, they can still bite. Watch this" He took a pencil from his pocket and put it in the Cheetah's mouth and wiggled it slightly. He touched a certain area and SNAP! The mouth closed and snapped the pencil in two. I couldn't believe it. The muscles in the mouth had been triggered and closed the mouth. It was so strong it could have taken my finger off. Something I have never forgotten, and I am grateful for being saved from a Cheetahs bite, even if it was dead.

The last one that really made an impression on me was. A Dolphin had died, and once again a post mortem was being carried out. Now we all know that Dolphins are mammals and not fish. But my inner brain wouldn't compute this properly when the vet cut it open to reveal red meat. My brain was saying white fish like texture but my eyes were seeing full on, red, cow like meat. It's obvious that it would be, but in a surreal way it seemed wrong. Just my weird brain having a moment that I thought was quite amusing. You learn so much when you're in the company of a vet.

Liam is laughing but finds this also very interesting. You don't get to see the inner workings of a Dolphin every day.

I guess one of the worst events to have been involved with has to be the culling of over 100 Rhesus Macaques after an outbreak of the Simian Herpes B virus. A devastating virus that can kill humans. Many monkeys are carriers of the disease but it lies dormant and doesn't always manifest itself. But on this occasion the whole troop tested positive and, as there was a risk of transmission to humans, the whole troop had to be put to sleep. Something that will stick with me for the rest of my life, and not in a good way. I feel for all those involved. At least three animal parks lost their entire troops in the year 2000. Let's hope we never have to do it again.

"That sounds dreadful. I am so sorry mate. I can't imagine being involved with such a thing." Liam sympathises.

CHAPTER 14

Vietnam

"So tell me about Vietnam?" Asks Liam. "Okay, but it's only a short one as it's a relatively new project." I told him.

Chào mừng bạn đến Viet nam. Welcome to Vietnam.

By now life has moved on. Having worked in Devon for many years at another animal park, an opportunity arose to be part of something very new. Yorkshire Wildlife Park, one of the newest animal collections in the UK, is expanding quickly. Brand new species that I have not worked with before and exciting new developments looked too good to pass up. Many of the management at the park were people with whom I have known and worked with for several years previously, so it was good to be working with them again.

So now I'm working for Yorkshire Wildlife Park. The park has done a lot of work around the world for conservation and supports projects and conservation charities via the Yorkshire Wildlife Park Foundation. I had the opportunity to get involved with an amazing project in Vietnam working alongside Wild Welfare and Animals Asia.

The Park has excellent ties with the charity group, 'Wild Welfare.' They unite zoos from all over the world with the aim to improve the welfare standards of all captive wild animals. They came to Yorkshire to give a presentation and explain what they did. I was very intrigued by this and was delighted to discover that they were looking for someone to be a point of contact for a zoo in Vietnam and to get involved with the project. Yorkshire wanted to send someone over to Vietnam, speak to the keepers and get hands on and make a real difference.

I jumped at this opportunity and I was delighted to discover, after a few interviews for suitability, that I was chosen to do it.

My role was essentially an animal husbandry and welfare advisor. As such I was to go to Vietnam and get involved with the keepers to advise and guide them on new ideas on how to improve the health and welfare of the animals in their care. This also included the building and renovations of new enclosures and discussing new ways of working with both animals and staff. This would then improve the living conditions of the animals who lived there.

My first visit was in July 2017. It was to be a fact finding mission and an introduction to the staff and animals at Hanoi Zoo. I joined the keepers in their every day routines such as cleaning, feeding and maintenance. I would sit with them at break times in order to get to know them. I also met with the directors and managers of the zoo to talk about ideas and discuss the conditions that the animals were living in and how we could make improvements for them. I wasn't there to tell them what to do. I was there to assist and present them with new ideas.

I soon gained a lot of trust from the staff and they were happy for me to join in with their work. They would laugh at me for my lack of Vietnamese, but I had an excellent interpreter called Thanh, so the language barrier was never an issue. Each day we would go out to see the animals and we would add, remove and rebuild furniture in several enclosures to liven up the space for what ever lived within it. Being able to show them what we did in the UK and to help them adapt our ideas was great fun. Even little things like changing or adding substrates could make a huge difference to a species. Substrates are the type of material on the floor of the enclosure. At Hanoi they were predominantly tiled floors. By changing it to grass, gravel, soil, sand or similar can have health benefits such as keeping claws trim, or a soft surface to keep feet healthy as well as offering new ways to present food by burying it or hiding it in rocks for the animal to search for in a more naturalistic way. We had lots of ideas on enrichment items and different ways to present food. In several cases the keepers would just throw food on the floor and walk away. We encouraged them to place food in different areas, inside logs, up a tree or hide it in a box. Anything that would make the animal search for it would improve on its curiosity and dexterity. Many animals forage for food so encouraging this behaviour can only be a good thing. When the keepers saw the changes in their animals behaviour they were delighted. The visiting public also enjoyed it and spent more time at each enclosure watching what the animal was doing because it was no longer asleep at the back of the enclosure due to boredom. The more the keepers did the more they got involved.

I also advised on veterinary issues. Having come across ailments familiar to them but having dealt with them from a western point of view, I was able to add to their repertoire. I also learnt from them and I saw how they would deal with issue. A truly fascinating learning experience for me.

On one occasion they were sedating seven Asian Black Bears and two Sun Bears in order to give them microchips and to health check them. This is a major operation. Nine Bears in one day is quite intense. They did the whole thing in one afternoon! Very efficient and very well done. They brought in experts from outside agencies and allowed me to be involved too. In the UK we would use a mechanical dart rifle to sedate the animal and we would never enter the enclosure until we were certain the animal was fully asleep. We would also complete the work on one animal before starting over on the next. At Hanoi Zoo they were using blow-pipes and a keeper would walk in with the animal before it went to sleep to keep an eye on it. While the staff were working on the first Bear the dart crew were already sedating the next Bear. Although a little alien to methods I have been involved with, I cannot deny that it was super efficient and cut the working time by half. This also reduced the time the animals had to stress. I have used a blow-pipe myself when I once sedated a Cheetah, so I know first hand how difficult it can be. These guys obviously did this regularly, and it showed. Perfect shots every time.

They are very limited by funds and they do have a very different outlook on animal welfare, but between us we can make a huge difference. They continue to contact me for ideas and advice on many different issues and between us we have made some real improvements.

Some of the projects were filmed and they enjoyed watching this back. I have seen that, since my visits, they are continuing to come up with new ideas and they are filming themselves doing it in order to share this with other zoos across the country. It's a slow process but at least progress is being made. Worth doing if it means that the animals gain a better life. Through these initiatives we can all make a difference. I am very pleased and lucky that I could be involved with it.

'Animals Asia' is a charitable organisation dedicated to improving the welfare of animals across Asia, particularly in campaigning to stop Bear bile farming. They are also heavily involved in the Hanoi Zoo project. They have staff in Vietnam who are available to assist at every level, including talking to government officials, and working at ground level. They are doing an amazing job and I am proud to have worked alongside them. They were integral in assisting with my communication with the staff and were very hands on with the builds and veterinary care. Without them I would have really struggled.

Lunch with the keepers at Hanoi Zoo.
Picture: © Colin Northcott.

CHAPTER 15

Miscellaneous and moves

While chatting with Liam I am getting bombarded with snippets of memories that have a place in so many areas. I thought I would place some of them here so you can have a read and hopefully enjoy.

Liam asks, "There is so much that's gone on in your life. I'm not surprised you have so many memories."

I do remember when I was called upon to trace a potential Wolf that had been sighted in the woods near the Safari Park. The first, and obvious, thing to do is to count your own animals to make sure they are all there. Once you have established the sighting is not yours you can then go and take a look. So I drove up to the last place it was seen and start to look for traces like tracks or faeces. I found nothing. No sign of it anywhere. So I drove back to the park. Ten minutes later a separate sighting is reported to us, so off I go again to look for it. Still nothing. This time I am still at the last sighting when I am called again with another report just half a mile from me. I hurry to the area and still I find nothing. This happened a further four times. Marking a map they did seem to correspond with an animal moving in a particular direction. Seven sightings in the same area from seven different sources must mean something is out there. Although I never did find out what it was. No further sightings were reported after this. It remains a mystery.

I also investigated several so called 'big cat' sightings around the area. None of them turned out to be a 'big cat.' In fact one of them was an Irish Wolfhound!

Once I was dropping off a load of manure at the muck heap. My colleague was with me. I am right handed and he is left handed. We were stood side by side when suddenly I felt a thump on the back of my hand. I looked down to see that his fork had gone straight through my hand and embedded itself in to the handle of the fork I was holding! The strangest thing was, I couldn't feel a thing. We pulled the prongs of his fork from the handle I was holding and removed it from my hand. Probably not the best thing to do, but that's what we did. I walked over to the office and announced that I needed to go to the hospital to have an injury checked out. The wound never bled and I still couldn't feel any pain. The nurse flushed it clean, gave me a tetanus, and wrapped my hand. I went back to work and carried on with my duties. Now i'm not acting all bravado. It simply never hurt so I just carried on. It missed any nerves and veins and went between the bones so it really didn't do any damage. Unlike the time the gate broke my foot.

The entrance to the Tiger enclosure was a hand operated gate that was covered with a solid panel. That meant that when the wind was blowing it was like trying to control a huge heavy kite, and it was over a cattle grid. On this particular day the wind was gusting hard. I waited for it to drop and I made a run for it to get it open. I slipped on the cattle grid and dropped my foot down the groove. At the same time the wind threw the gate back at me and straight over my foot jamming it tight in the grid. I was completely stuck and in great pain. To make matters worse I had left my two-way radio in the lLand Rover so I couldn't call for help, and I knew that no one else was due up to that area for another hour at least. I guess through fear and pain and adrenalin I used my free foot to push the gate back off my trapped foot. It took several goes and was very painful, but I managed to get free. I hobbled back to the vehicle and drove down to the office. I fully expected to go to the hospital but instead the boss said, "You've probably sprained your ankle. Go and man the towers if it hurts to walk." Surprised at this I did what I was asked. That evening I drove myself to hospital and they confirmed that I had indeed broken the heel bone and wrapped me up accordingly. The next day I arrived at work on crutches.

Liam says, "I bet he was a bit embarrassed that he didn't send you to hospital earlier wasn't he?" My reply was, "No, he wasn't at all!"

"Babies." I said. "Go on." Liam replies. There were so many babies born at all the parks I have worked for. Sometimes they require help. Whether they have been abandoned or orphaned there is often a need to help them out. Sometimes hand rearing can lead to troublesome adults. If they have been raised by humans they don't always have the same bond with their own kind and can lose a position in a hierarchy of a species which can result in rejection or death. They can also become imprinted on humans and rather than keeping a healthy distance from them, they instead actively seek out human attention. Not good if it's a Tiger or Lion. But if you're asked to save a life by your peers then that's what you do. This is usually only the case if the animal in question is an endangered species. However, one of the new borns I have helped was a naughty little Hamadryas Baboon. Looked after by another I assisted for a short time. Such a cute little thing that would wee all over the place! You had to be on your guard with the tissues at the ready. He was eventually reintroduced and accepted by the troop and grew up to be an integral player.

I also remember helping with some Lion cubs. Many, in fact, over my career. After about six months they are definitely too much trouble to handle. They are usually reintroduced much earlier, or we re-homed to another collection. Great fun, but they can be dangerous. I did revive a dead cub once. I gave it mouth to mouth and it survived.

A Tapir we named 'Lutador,' or 'Luta' for short, was breach born and died a few hours later. I managed to bring life back to him and I also managed to collect milk from his mother by milking her as you would a cow or goat, and fed it to him. Between myself and the other keepers we successfully reintroduced him back to his mother and he grew up to be a strong, if sometimes naughty, adult and now lives at a great facility in Norfolk. By chance one of the keepers involved in raising him later went to the same zoo and continued to look after him. He hopes to be a dad himself one day.

A Rhea chick, that was discarded as an unviable egg, hatched just in time before being disposed of with a group of infertile eggs. I raised him to adulthood and he would walk with me around the park. He now lives a happy life in a facility in Somerset.

Several Mara that needed assistance to survive after being flooded out of their burrow and left for dead. In fact, one of them was dead and I was able to revive it and nurse it to become a strong adult. They also live a good life in a new facility.

A Painted Dog pup that was the only one of the litter to survive but it sadly passed away after just a few days. Even when we lose them we can still learn from them.

Even wildlife sometimes needs a hand. I have raised Hedgehogs and kept them going for wild release. A little bird that was handed to me as a fledgling I raised to adulthood. Turned out to be a female Sparrow and she would visit me throughout the summer. If I left my front door open she would fly in and sit on my head. One day I saw her join a group of wild Sparrows in the trees opposite my home and she flew off with the flock.

All these encounters leave an impression on me and I have learnt from each one of them. Hopefully making me a better keeper, although as I get older my memory isn't as sharp as it was!

So many things have changed over the years. I have now worked in five separate facilities and seen the changes happening in front of me. Keeping up with them is difficult, but very important in order to give the very best care that the animals deserve. No one owns the animals. We are custodians. They have no voice so we have to speak for them. Keepers all over the world work tirelessly to ensure that the animals they look after get the best possible care. I think the human race has done enough damage to the world and to all who share it. Earth does not belong to us. We are just tenants who share it with the rest of the animal kingdom. We owe it to the others to restore some of the balance so everything can live a full and happy life. Free from hunger. Free from pain. Free to live their own lives. Animal parks around the world play a vital role in the preservation of so many endangered species. If it wasn't for these facilities so many more creatures would have become extinct. You can support them by just by visiting. You will be amazed at what you see.

To date, at the time of writing this, I have worked with over 150 species, not including the extras in Vietnam, and assisted with a further 15 or so. From Orca to Agouti, or Armadillo to Elephant. It's been a real blast. And the ride continues.

Now living and working in Yorkshire with the animals, I love to wander around the countryside and watch the wildlife doing their thing. Animals oblivious to all the crap that we have caused with climate change. To see Deer roaming is a real treat. I see rare birds and get a real buzz. My home has also been home to several wild creatures that live amongst the infrastructure, including Whiskered Bats who lived in the roof space. I am so happy that they had chosen to live with me. Nature is a wonderful thing, without which we could not survive ourselves.

Enjoy it. But don't destroy it.

Thank you to Liam Smith for the chat and sparking a lot of very happy memories. We drink up and leave. We did pay for our meals before we left of course!

I leave you with a few pictures of interest. Enjoy.

Lion cub. West Midland Safari Park.
Picture: © Colin Northcott

Meeting a Gorilla at Twycross Zoo. Circa 1990.
Picture: © Colin Northcott.

Feeding Cheetahs at Windsor Safari Park. Circa 1989.
Picture © Colin Northcott.

Wolf Cub at West Midland Safari Park.
Picture © Colin Northcott.

Feeding a Tiger at Windsor Safari Park. Circa 1991.
Picture © Colin Northcott.

Feeding the Lions at Windsor Safari Park.
Circa 1991. Picture: © Colin Northcott.

Savannah sunset. West Midland Safari Park.
Picture: © Colin Northcott.

Thank you for reading and I wish you all well.

CREDITS

I'd like to give a special mention to the following for their involvement in the Vietnam project:

Yorkshire Wildlife Park:
Yorkshire Wildlife Park Foundation:
John Minion.
Cheryl Williams MBE.
Debbie Porter.
Andy Watson.

Wild Welfare:
David Neale.
Georgina Groves.

Animals Asia:
Dionne Slagter.
Thanh Nguyen.
Do Thanhhuong.

Hanoi Zoo:
Danh Cường and all the keepers.

And to everyone else involved with the project.
Long may they continue to make a difference.

About the Author

Author, Colin. With a young Mara he hand reared.
Picture: © Colin Northcott.

Colin was born in Cardiff, Wales. He moved to Plymouth at the age of 5 when his parents moved there for work. He first discovered an interest in animals when he visited what was then the Central Park Zoo in Plymouth, now closed. Seeing the animals fascinated him, and so the spark was ignited. He moved to Somerset when he was 12 and started to take an interest in the local wildlife, quickly becoming an amateur ornithologist and joining the Young Ornithologists Club, (YOC), and then the Royal Society for the Protection of Birds,

(RSPB). A few years after leaving school he finally secured his first Zoo Keeper position at Windsor Safari Park.

After the closure of Windsor he progressed his career by moving on to work for several other Zoological collections around the country including West Midlands Safari Park and Woburn Safari Park. His work was further boosted by becoming a consultant in Animal Care and Husbandry to Vietnamese Zoos on behalf of the Yorkshire Wildlife Park and the Yorkshire Wildlife Park Foundation. Now, with over 33 years in the industry under his belt, and still counting, he shows no sign of stopping and will continue to provide the best he can for the animals he cares so much for.

When not at work he can be found roaming the countryside with binoculars in hand and a camera around his neck searching for those elusive native species.

He also likes tea...... a lot!

Printed by Amazon Italia Logistica S.r.l.
Torrazza Piemonte (TO), Italy

42127525R00067